PSYCHO-ANALYSIS
AS HISTORY

PSYCHO-ANALYSIS
AS HISTORY

Negation and
Freedom in Freud

MICHAEL S. ROTH

CORNELL UNIVERSITY PRESS

ITHACA AND LONDON

First published 1987 by Cornell University Press.

International Standard Book Number 0-8014-1957-3
Library of Congress Catalog Card Number 86-29192
Printed in the United States of America
Librarians: Library of Congress cataloging information
appears on the last page of the book.

The paper in this book is acid-free and meets the guidelines for permanence and durability of the Committee on Production Guidelines for Book Longevity of the Council on Library Resources.

For Lila Roth and Joseph Roth
and for Cayuga

Contents

Preface

   In order to comprehend Freud's contribution to,
or effect on, modern culture, one must understand what kind
of theory psycho-analysis is. This book will present Freud's
work as a theory of history, showing his contribution as a
framework through which we can make sense of our pasts.
The theory aims to help us negate elements of this past by
coming to terms with them. Negation (*Aufhebung*) does not
make the past disappear; on the contrary, it allows us to live
with a past we have grasped. The result of this acknowledging is a kind of freedom.

   This book does not attempt to provide a total or even to-
talizing interpretation of psycho-analysis. I will not join the
great debate between those who think, as Freud himself often
thought, that psycho-analysis tries to be a science like the
natural sciences, and those who think, as Freud sometimes
thought, that psycho-analysis puts the insights of poets and
philosophers into another form. Instead, I will offer a partial
reading of Freud, but a reading that makes sense of what is
most central in psycho-analysis.

   I have aimed to show throughout this essay how psycho-
analysis provides a framework for us to make sense of our
pasts; a hermeneutic according to which we construct a
reading of the meaning and directions of our pasts with which
we can live, or with which we can change our lives. Thus, by

calling psycho-analysis a theory of history, I am making no claims about Freud's connections to the contemporary genre of psychohistory. Instead, I have located psycho-analysis in that field in which writers have tried to make meaning out of memory in the service of a present moving significantly into a future.

Calling psycho-analysis a theory of history does not, of course, solve many of the important theoretical problems in Freud's work. It does, however, define the area in which these problems occur. "History" is used here, and throughout this book, to refer to the history of the individual. The connection between such individual history and the history of groups will be the subject of Section III.

In my explication of its most crucial theoretical developments, I try to show that psycho-analysis as Freud conceived it is first and foremost a theory of history aimed at establishing in the person a more complete consciousness than had previously existed. Such a consciousness is a precondition of freedom. The psycho-analytic concept of "sublimation" is most generally associated with the capacity to redirect one's life, freely, toward specific goals. I shall underline the difficulties inherent in this concept and, given the meaning that psycho-analysis can make from a person's history, show the possibilities for self-conscious change which are established by the transference phenomenon.

The reader must constantly keep in mind that nothing is being said in this work about Freud's personal views on history, philosophy, politics, science, or, for that matter, about his personal views on psycho-analysis. The only concern here is with Freud's theory.

Theory must be distinguished not only from the biography of its originator, but from therapy as well. That is, the discussions in this work are directly related not to questions of therapeutic efficacy but only to the theory of psycho-analysis in Freud's writings. The distinction between theory and therapy is more difficult to maintain in the second section of this work, especially in regard to the transference phenomenon, a part of therapy. Even there, however, I am concerned with

10

Freud's theory—in this case, the theory of therapy—and not with therapeutic efficacy as such.

The interpretation presented here is of psycho-analysis as Freud developed it, and I write the name of his theory in the old-fashioned hyphenated form; "psychoanalysis" is used in reference to Freud's professional followers.

Most of this essay is explication, and not deductive argument. I have chosen this method of presentation because it more readily allows, to use Charcot's phrase, "the signs to speak for themselves." Freud's theory is a theory of history and does not need any special development to become one. Of course, any explication is also an interpretation, but when the material is seen in the way that I have presented it, this interpretation can be viewed as a part of the theory itself and not an outright addition to it. That said, what follows does not attempt to provide an account of all the possibilities that Freud's writings create. Instead, I have developed a reading of these materials that makes sense of them within a limited horizon in which psycho-analysis emerges clearly as a theory of history.

An account of the political implications of psycho-analysis must be grounded in a close reading of Freud's theory of the individual. Since the title of this book mentions freedom and history, the reader may be surprised to find the bulk of it devoted to detailed discussions of the major theoretical developments in Freud's work, and not to his speculations on group psychology. These developments must be "worked through," however, if the relevance of psycho-analysis to any theory of group dynamics and of politics is to be understood.

Psycho-analysis has a large technical vocabulary that is often difficult to penetrate and understand. I have tried in this work to use nontechnical, more generally accessible language whenever possible, a task made more difficult by the fact that many ordinary words have been "technicalized" by psycho-analysis. I have tried to avoid such words, and the reader may assume that my language is not used in any specialized (professional psychoanalytic) sense except where such a context is obvious.

I have chosen to use the male pronoun in a generic sense ("he" meaning "he or she"). I apologize for this use, though at present it seems to me the most workable formulation. The reader may assume that the pronoun "he" refers to either the male or female, except in the discussion of the Oedipus complex and sex differences.

Many people gave me intellectual and personal support while I worked on this project. I am grateful to Adolf Grünbaum, Louis Mink, Philip Pomper, Bennett E. Roth, Carl E. Schorske, Jerrold Seigel, and Hayden White for their scholarly assistance. I especially thank Joel Fineman for discussing the project with me in its very early stages. My conversations with Victor Gourevitch about Hegel and about psycho-analysis have been invaluable for me, as were Richard Vann's encouragement and assistance in the first revisions of the manuscript. I completed much of the project as a Junior Fellow at the Center for Humanities at Wesleyan University and am thankful for the opportunity I had to work in that setting. The book was completed with the assistance of Scripps College, which provided me with funds that enabled me to concentrate on the final preparations of the manucript. William Jones gave me very useful bibliographic assistance for these preparations, and Clara Min, Ingrid Dahlberg, and Kristin Wagner worked to get the manuscript into final shape. Kay Scheuer has been a helpful, patient, and intelligent editor.

Henry Abelove of the History Department at Wesleyan University helped guide this project at its inception. He has been a source of personal support and intellectual inspiration throughout the time I have devoted to it. His painstakingly close readings of early drafts and his comments on them have been extremely valuable to me.

Finally, my thanks to Laurence Roth, for her recent doubts about history, and for her more abiding faith in destiny. And to Jeremy, for helping us find joy in both.

Claremont, California   MICHAEL S. ROTH

PSYCHO-ANALYSIS
AS HISTORY

Introduction

A theory that concentrates on the past, psychoanalysis has been viewed as conceiving mature (post-pubescent) human nature to be essentially unchangeable, as allowing for no radical changes in the very period when a person has the consciousness to desire such changes. To put this view in positive terms: changes in the years after childhood occur only within the boundaries, or laws of personality, set in childhood.

Freud has most typically been seen as the apogee of the liberal tradition. That is—in contrast to the work of more radical theorists—his work has been viewed as showing the possibilities for moderate changes in the way people go about their lives. This prudence of aim is best expressed by Freud's own therapeutic goals: to transform hysterical misery into common unhappiness.[1] Indeed, the very nature of the therapeutic effect seems to preclude any talk of profound change or radical action, since implicit in therapy is the notion of adaptation. If the neurotic is the symptom of a sick society, as Freud's work sometimes seems to tell us, then psychoanalysis appears to be the effort merely to coordinate the

[1] Sigmund Freud and Joseph Breuer, *Studies on Hysteria*, in *The Standard Edition of the Complete Psychological Works of Sigmund Freud*, ed. and trans. James Strachey et al. (London: Hogarth, 1953–74) (hereafter *SE*), II, 305.

15

needs of society and the individual; to mediate between the two so that some of the rational needs of each can be met. This idea of a balance between the desires of the individual and the demands of the society, which seems to underlie almost the entire corpus of Freud's writings, is quite far from the idea of radical action, in that it calls for a moderation of desires and demands by degree and not by kind. Many modern psychotherapists and "radical psychologists" have consistently attacked this aspect of Freud's theory.

Freud's critics, however, as well as most of his followers, have failed to follow through on their analysis of this theme of balance, which in fact contains most of the potential for understanding real change that Freud's work offers. In his earliest writings the concept of balance is centered on the resolution of the contradictions between the desires of the person and his place in the external world. In *The Project for a Scientific Psychology* contradiction is seen as the impetus of both thought and action.[2] As the contradictions become more profound and more painful, the amount of thought and action necessary for their resolution becomes greater. In much the same way that Marxism does, psycho-analysis points to the fact that if the contradictions between the individual's desires and the group's needs become great enough, the person's activity will have to be deeply radical to achieve the necessary resolution. At the same time, psycho-analysis emphasizes that radical activity will occur only if the sacrifice needed to reach such a resolution is outweighed by the potential gratification of the radical change.

The awareness of these contradictions is achieved through an understanding of the history of their development. The contradictions are themselves the impetus of analysis—they are conflicts that cause pain—and not situations that hypothetically exist in the future. The actual presence of conflict is fundamental to psycho-analysis, and indeed, the discipline is limited to the study of the *history* of conflict. Psycho-

---

[2] *SE*, I, 361, 386–387.

analysis cannot extend its exploration of the past into a vision of the future. That psycho-analysis is limited to the past
makes the claim that Freud's work can add anything to our
understanding of negation and the potential for future change
problematic, but it also touches on the point at which the
concept of freedom in his work is most profound. Psycho-
analysis is a *historical science* in that its fundamental theoretical tenet is that the individual—and by analogy the group—
can act with a degree of freedom that is achieved through an
understanding, a working through, of his past. Psycho-analysis is a *theory of history* because it develops a grid through
which certain periods of a person's past are given an extraordinary place in the perspective on the present; also, because
it views certain types of action and thought as having a greater
impact on the succeeding development of the person's history than others. All this analysis, however, ends with the
present. Psycho-analysis is no longer a depth psychology if
it becomes predictive. It claims our attention as a general
social theory when it pursues the analysis of its object, the
unconscious and its manifestations, creating the opportunity
for the analysand to make a decisive break with the past.
Psycho-analysis cannot compel the person to make such a
break; he can continue in the patterns he had established up
until the analysis, or he can find a way to mediate between
the past and his desires in the present. Indeed, such a mediation will be the most likely outcome. Nonetheless, the
possibility for radical change is created. The analysand is in
a psychological position to explore that possibility.

Several problems in my description of Freud's work have
already become apparent. The first is that the emphasis I put
on the end of analysis in the present appears to be inconsis-
tent with the idea of using acuteness of contradictions to
predict when change will occur. The function of contradiction in the theory, however, is not predictive, but only to be
an aid in the interpretation of the choice made at the end of
analysis. To predict this choice in any concrete temporal sense
would involve the measurement of "pain," "gratification," and

"sacrifice," and such measurement is not within the scope of psycho-analysis.[3]

Furthermore, how can a theory of the unconscious be relevant to freedom and change when it concentrates on—or is limited to—the "subjective" dimension of the person? Also, if psycho-analysis moves from the individual to the group, it does so by way of analogy only, and to label even an individual "free," or to say that he has the capacity for profound change without an understanding of the constraints of his context is problematic, to say the least. An objection to Freud's thought based on these difficulties would be a serious one, since any discussion of the political implications of psycho-analysis would rest on the strength of the analogy between the individual and the group. One of the goals of this work is to show that the basis for such an analogy exists in Freud's exploration of the individual and that, indeed, the application of the theory of psycho-analysis to the group can be a true development of this original exploration. In the last section of this book some analogies at the group level are detailed.

This essay is made up of three parts. The first section, "Interpretation and History," will show the necessity of reading Freud's work as interpretive of the past, rather than as predictive of the future. It will do so by examining three of the crucial theoretical strands of psycho-analysis: the theory of dreams (especially the dreamwork and dream interpretation); the theory of repression and its symptoms or signs; the theory of infantile sexuality and its stages of development. The second section, "Acknowledging and Freedom," examines two ways, sublimation and the transference, in which the individual comes to terms with his history—a history in which dreams, repression, and sexuality have an extraordinary place. "Acknowledging and Freedom" will show the theoretical basis for the freedom found in an apprehension

[3]This is not to argue that psycho-analytic presuppositions cannot be tested, only that they cannot be tested in psycho-analysis. See Adolf Grünbaum, *The Foundations of Psychoanalysis* (Berkeley, 1984), passim.

of the transference phenomenon. A person conscious of the contradictions in his actions, thoughts, and history, as well as of the sacrifice that would be necessary to resolve them, would have open before him the possibility of negating that history, because he would have an understanding of the past, of dreams, and of the work necessary to create a future that would be connected with, without being a repetition of, the past.

The third section will discuss some analogies at the group level to the theory of dreams, the theory of repression, and the theories of sublimation and the transference. In my development of these analogies it will become clear that psycho-analysis is not necessarily confined to a theory of the individual, and that it can be valuable as a vehicle for insight into the processes of the group. The insight into a history and the possibilities for its negation are not lost at the group level.

The theory of dreams is one of the defining features of psycho-analysis, as well as one of the central areas of difficulty for the development and understanding of the theory as a whole. Freud's approach to the dream is the prototype of his perspective on everything that psycho-analysis examines. "Anyone who has failed to explain the origin of dream-images can scarcely hope to understand phobias, obsessions or delusions or to bring a therapeutic influence to bear on them," he writes in the preface to the first edition of *The Interpretation of Dreams*.[4] And later he notes that dream theory "occupies a special place in the history of psycho-analysis and marks a turning point; it was with it that analysis took the step from being a psychotherapeutic procedure to being a depth psychology. Since then, too, the theory of dreams has remained what is most characteristic and peculiar about the young science."[5]

It is with the theory of dreams, then, that any investigation of the interpretive strategies of psycho-analysis must begin.

---

[4] *SE*, IV, xxiii.
[5] *New Introductory Lectures on Psycho-Analysis*, *SE*, XXII, 7.

My purpose here, however, is not to explicate the dream theory as a whole, but rather to understand the ways it makes meaning out of signs of the past in the present. Therefore, I shall concentrate on the method of dream interpretation and the dreamwork, chapters 2 and 6 of *The Interpretation of Dreams*. The hermeneutic quality of dream theory will become evident.

No less important than dream theory for psycho-analysis is the concept of repression. It is the essential dynamic element for understanding the way internal conflict—which the dreamwork examined in part—is expressed in external signs, that is, in symptoms. "The theory of repression," Freud wrote, "is the corner-stone on which the whole structure of psycho-analysis rests."[6] It is through the discovery and analysis of repression that psycho-analysis evolves into a systematic account of the unconscious and its effects on both normal and pathological living, rather than remaining merely a technique of dream interpretation. That is not to say that one followed from the other, but rather that the investigation of dream processes, which increased in importance for Freud as a result of his discovery of the problem of repression ("knowing yet not knowing"), became relevant to waking life because of the universal presence of repression in humans. Indeed, the defense mechanisms as a whole are the crux of psycho-analysis' understanding of desire and the possibilities for freedom.[7] The questions whether some degree of repression is necessary for the workings of consciousness, and how repression relates to sublimation and the transference will be important here. We shall examine the connection between repression and freedom, and whether repression *necessarily* entails manifestations of any particular sort. Its relationship to the dreamwork will also be explored, since the

[6] "On the History of the Psycho-Analytic Movement," *SE*, xiv, 16.

[7] The relationship between repression and the other defense mechanisms will not be fully discussed in this work. Repression here is viewed as a distinctive mechanism of defense, and not merely one of many strategies of defending the ego.

latter provides an explanation of how unconscious material becomes manifest.

The psycho-analytic theory of infantile sexuality has been the point at which the popular imagination has encountered Freud and where most people professionally concerned with psychology have rejected him. This part of the theory is no less important than the two just discussed for the formation of psycho-analysis; indeed, it is intimately bound up with them. That is not to say that psycho-analysis "attributes everything to sexuality," but rather that one of Freud's major findings was the extraordinary place that sexuality has in the history of the person: that it sets the paradigm for the person's relationship to all objects of perception.[8] Sexuality forms the material base of the psyche as conceived by psycho-analysis; rather than being the point where analysis starts in a mechanical way, it is the base to which the analysis leads, and analysis can go no further when desire is conceived as physiological need. Psycho-analysis does not proceed beyond the mental; it has as its limit the psychological manifestations of the biological. Even the drives are considered as representations of biological impulses and not the impulses themselves. If psycho-analysis were to pass into biology it would cease to be an instrument through which persons can initiate change through the acknowledgement, the apprehension, of their history. When psycho-analysis operates within its domain, it is only an instrument for understanding the mental, and any transformation that occurs is through the understanding that the analysand achieves.

These will be the focal points of Section I, "Interpretation and History." Freud's system of interpretation, it will become clear, makes sense of the present by seeing it as containing the significance of the past. Freud does have a theory of the ways in which unconscious material manifests itself, how certain kinds of experiences lead to particular conflicts. This

[8]See especially, Freud, "On Narcissism: An Introduction," *SE*, xiv, 73–104, and the description of primary process in *The Interpretation of Dreams*, *SE*, v, 599–611.

21

theory works, however, only when there is present a sign which is the product of conflict; the analysis works backward from that given point. The hysterical symptom is a historical sign, the object of interpretation; the unconscious conflict is apprehended only through the analysis of the way the analysand expresses the symptom. The reversal of the process is impossible *within psycho-analytic inquiry properly so-called* because without the existence of the sign there would be nothing to analyze, to interpret. Psycho-analysis is not concerned, then, with retrodiction, but with historical reconstruction.[9] By "historical reconstruction" I mean not a representation of the past *as it really was,* but a reconfiguration of it in such a way as to give meaning and direction to the present.[10]

[9] Many writers have noted the ways in which psycho-analysis functions in regard to history: Paul Ricoeur, *Freud and Philosophy: An Essay on Interpretation,* trans. Denis Savage (New Haven, 1970), pp. 362–363, 374–375; Jean-Paul Sartre, *Being and Nothingness: An Essay on Phenomenological Ontology,* trans. Hazel E. Barnes (New York, 1956), p. 458; Jacques Lacan, "The Function of Language in Psychoanalysis," in *The Language of the Self,* trans. Anthony Wilden (New York, 1968), pp. 23, 82; Kenneth Burke, *Language as Symbolic Action: Essays on Life, Literature, and Method* (Berkeley, 1966), pp. 67–68, and *A Grammar of Motives* (Berkeley, 1969), pp. 431–432; Michel Foucault, *Mental Illness and Psychology,* trans. Alan Sheridan (New York, 1976), pp. 19, 33–43. This list is by no means exhaustive. On psycho-analysis and historical investigation, see, for example, John Klauber, "On the Use of Historical and Scientific Method in Psychoanalysis," *IJP,* 49, (1968), 80–88; W. Novey, *The Second Look: The Reconstruction of Personal History in Psychiatry and Psychoanalysis* (Baltimore, 1968); Hans Loewald, *Psychoanalysis and the History of the Individual* (New Haven, 1980); Roy Schafer, "Narration in the Psychoanalytic Dialogue," *Critical Inquiry,* 7 (1981), 29–54; Peter Gay, *Freud for Historians* (Oxford, 1985).

[10] On reconstruction in analysis, see Phylis Greenacre, "On Reconstruction," *Journal of the American Psychoanalytic Association,* 23 (1975), 693–712; and, especially, Harold P. Blum, "The Value of Reconstruction in Adult Psychoanalysis," *IJP,* 61 (1980), 39–52. On the fundamentally poetic aspects of the historian's "reconfiguration of the past" see Hayden White's use of the notion of "emplotment" in *Metahistory: The Historical Imagination in Nineteenth Century Europe* (Baltimore, 1973), passim, and his "The Politics of Historical Interpretation: Discipline and De-Sublimation," *Critical Inquiry,* 9 (1982), 113–137. See also Dominick LaCapra, "Rethinking Intellectual History and Reading Texts," *History and Theory,* 19 (1980), 245–276, and my "Foucault's 'History of the Present'," *History and Theory,* 20 (1981), 32–46.

It has perhaps already become clear that the reading of Freud in this book will depend on some form of dialectical understanding of the relation of a meaningful history to the present. This dependence situates my interpretation between the biologistic (and often American) understanding of psycho-analysis,[11] and the post-structuralist (and often French) return to and critique of Freud.[12] There are certainly elements in psycho-analysis that lend themselves to a biologistic appropriation. My purpose is not to deny Freud's connection to this view of the mind, but to suggest an alternative— and more comprehensive—interpretation. His work can be meaningfully understood without recourse to the idea of a "theory of history," but I shall show the dimensions of significance that are uncovered when this idea is seen to inform the major concepts of his theory.

These dimensions of significance, however, insofar as they are tied to a dialectical understanding of historical change, are vulnerable to the post-structuralist critique of dialectical negation, historical continuity, and the whole idea of making meaning out of change over time. I shall not in this book attempt to answer these criticisms, since in order to do so one would have to show in detail how structuralism and post-structuralism have developed as a reaction against a Hegelian philosophy of history. By showing the ways in which psycho-analysis makes sense as a theory of history, I shall establish the *preconditions* for understanding how it is related to much of contemporary theory's discourse on and about history generally. A full treatment of post-structuralism's impact on and development out of theories of history would be the subject for another book.[13]

[11] See, for example, Frank Sulloway, *Freud: Biologist of the Mind* (New York, 1979).

[12] See, for example, the later works of Jacques Lacan, and Gilles Deleuze and Felix Guattari, *L'Anti-Oedipe* (Paris, 1972).

[13] The connection of structuralism and post-structuralism to a Hegelian philosophy of history would be crucial in this regard. On the development of the latter in France, see my "Knowing and History: The Resurgence of French Hegelianism from the 1930's through the Post-War Period" (Ph.D. diss., Princeton University, 1983); and my "A Problem of Recognition: Alex-

In Section I it will become clear that Freud had what we can call a dialectical understanding of development. That is, early stages are not merely left behind in the push toward maturity; they remain crucial components of our being in the world. The "negation" *(Aufhebung)* of an earlier stage does not mean the disappearance of that stage, but rather its preservation in some other form. This understanding of development has been obscured in contemporary psychoanalysis by the debate between those who think interpretation is primarily genetic and those who think it should be focused, for the most part, on the "here and now." According to the understanding of development to be presented in Section I, the here and now always already contains the past. All genetic interpretations should be conceived, then, in terms of the "history of the present." Similarly, here-and-now interpretations that presuppose a psycho-analytic conception of development would point in some form to the significance of the analysand's history.

Also important to psycho-analytic reconstruction are the concept of overdetermination and the gaps that the theory postulates. Overdetermination may preclude the creation of a chain of causal determinants that would take into account all factors because criteria for sufficient causality would be almost impossible to establish. The gaps in interpretation are due not only to the always incomplete nature of inquiry (which is, after all, not specific to psycho-analysis), but to the very nature of the unconscious itself, which can be known only through its manifestations, never directly. As Freud remarks:

> Unconscious processes only become cognizable by us under the conditions of dreaming and neurosis—that is to say, when the processes of the higher, *Pcs.* [preconscious] system are set back to an earlier stage by being lowered (by regression). In themselves they cannot be cognized.[14]

---

andre Kojève and the End of History," *History and Theory*, 24 (1985), 293–306.

[14] "The Unconscious," *SE*, xiv, 187.

There is often a passage in even the most thoroughly inter-preted dream which has to be left obscure. . . . This is the dream's navel, the spot where it reaches down into the un-known. The dream-thoughts to which we are led by interpre-tation cannot, from the nature of things, have any definite end-ings.[15]

The gap left unbridged by analysis is the point at which the analysand must choose how to act, given the meaning of his history. As a system of interpretation psycho-analysis not only makes the analysand's choice meaningful; it also makes it possible, for a choice that takes place without understanding would be no choice at all.

The second part of this work, "Acknowledging and Free-dom," will deal with two forms in which that choice is made through psycho-analysis: sublimation and transference. Both these processes are important to the theory as a whole, but each has a status somewhat different from the first three top-ics considered.

It is difficult to capture the meaning of sublimation in Freud. Sublimation is the process through which the "higher activ-ities of man"—by this Freud usually means intellectual and artistic activities—derive their energy from the sexual in-stincts. "The sexual instinct," he writes, "is particularly well fitted to make contributions of this kind since it is endowed with a capacity for sublimation: that is, it has the power to replace its immediate aim by other aims which may be val-ued more highly and which are not sexual."[16] The concept of sublimation is one of the chief means by which psycho-analysis becomes relevant to a theory of culture. In this es-say, the concept has a pivotal position: it is one of the major means by which the conflict between the desires of the in-dividual and the demands of society is cast into sharp relief. Indeed, commentators on Freud interested in the social con-tent of psycho-analysis have focused on sublimation as the

[15] *The Interpretation of Dreams, SE,* v, 525.
[16] *Leonardo Da Vinci and a Memory of His Childhood, SE,* xi, 78.

key to the adaptation of individual desire to social constraints. Depending on their own preoccupations, they have either applauded Freud's realism or criticized his conservatism manifested through his understanding of this process.

Chapter 4 will present a critical account of sublimation as a vehicle for acknowledging the contradictions in the present by coming to terms with one's history. It will then examine the transference as a process through which this acknowledging can take place and lead to possibilities for change. Not that transference love is in itself a qualitatively new way of being; it certainly does not manifest a radically changed way of life. In fact, it is the very opposite of such a life, since it displays the repetitions, defenses, and frustrations that characterize the "pathological" facets of "normal" living. It is by being this manifestation, though, that the transference offers the analysand the prospects of negation, that is, of freedom through the creative acknowledging of one's history.

The transference phenomenon is both essential and dangerous to the process of the analytic treatment. Freud noted in "Dynamics of Transference" that "transference in the analytic treatment invariably appears to us in the first instance as the strongest weapon of the resistance."[17] Elsewhere he remarked, "If we succeed, as we usually can, in enlightening the patient on the true nature of the phenomena of transference, we shall have struck a powerful weapon out of the hand of his resistance and shall have converted dangers into gains."[18] The phenomenon is characterized by the analysand's redirecting his libidinal cathexes, which have been either frustrated or repressed, onto the analyst. The transference always has a sexual content.[19] It is through this relationship with the analyst that the person becomes aware of the patterns through which he has been acting on and per-

[17] *SE*, xii, 104.
[18] *An Outline of Psycho-Analysis*, *SE*, xxiii, 177.
[19] Freud, *On the History of the Psycho-Analytic Movement*, *SE*, xiv, 12.

ceiving the world—if these ways of acting and perceiving play a role in *unconscious conflict*—for the transference is not a way in which a person can step outside of his entire existence and understand it. Rather, it enables him to come to see the unconscious conflicts that underlie his activity revealed in an intersubjective situation.

The transference phenomenon relates back to the concept of contradiction that was stressed above. Only ideas and feelings that are in a state of contradiction would become apparent in the transference—unconscious forces that are in opposition to one another or to something else in consciousness.[20] Significant change would take place as a result of this relationship with the analyst only if the conditions that brought the person to the analytic situation involved contradictions painful enough to warrant the sacrifice necessary to make the radical resolution. Such a change could not be imposed from without by the analyst, or from the standpoint of an ideology that dogmatically demanded change without understanding the psychical dynamics, and the suffering, inherent in resolution.

The transference relationship manifests the contradictions between desire and the reality of the present as well as the difficulties inherent in change, since many of the desires are infantile impulses. The interpretation of the history of the present that is at the core of psycho-analytic theory enables the analysand to apprehend the meaning of the manifestation, to apprehend the ways in which his history conditions his present. With this knowledge analysis ends; the subject is left with the freedom to act in a self-conscious way. In order to describe more fully the freedom found at the end of psycho-analysis, I explore certain aspects of Hegel's concept of freedom, investigating Hegel's philosophy not in itself, but only for the illumination of Freud's goal of analysis—freedom based on self-consciousness.

Underscoring the importance of freedom found through

---

[20] Freud, "Analysis Terminable and Interminable," *SE*, xxiii, 230–234.

the transference raises the question of psycho-analysis's relevance to an understanding of group dynamics. Section III will pursue this question by showing that the application of psycho-analysis to the group level points to the possibilities of an analogous acknowledging and reconstruction of history. *Group Psychology and the Analysis of the Ego* will be examined in detail to show some of the ways psycho-analysis sheds light on certain key processes in the dynamics of group formation and maintenance. I will discuss other texts as well, to underscore the position that the investigation of the group is an elaboration of psycho-analysis consistent with its most important theoretical developments at the level of the individual.

Psycho-analysis can add to our understanding of the possibilities for change only through its theory of the history of the group and the individual. If it were used to *predict the content of change* it would be distorted into something that would only vaguely resemble Freud's work. Psycho-analytic theory, much like the transference phenomenon itself, is capable only of bringing into consciousness the contradictions that can lead to change. Freud's work points to the creation of a sensibility that comprehends the contradictions of its existence and the effort necessary to resolve them. In this way, Freud's work contributes to enabling the creation of freedom through self-consciousness, which may indeed be essential if change is to be distinguished from repetition.

There have, of course, been interpretations of Freud that have viewed his work as an important ingredient in a theory of (or speculation about) a radical restructuring of social relations. All such interpretations must come to terms with Freud's own pessimism about the prospects for that sort of change. The following pages may be regarded as an exploration into the depths of that pessimism: an exploration into the prospects for its negation. This path is the path of psycho-analysis itself. "Not in any beyond," said Freud, "but here on earth most men live in a hell: Schopenhauer has seen this very well. My knowledge, my theories and my methods have the goal of making men conscious of this hell so that they can free themselves from it."[21]

[21] Freud, cited by Helmut Dahmer in a review of B. Gortz, *Erinnerungen an Sigmund Freud*, in *Psyche*, 24 (1970), 132 (from Russell Jacoby, *Social Amnesia: A Critique of Conformist Psychology from Adler to Lang* [Boston, 1975], 119).

INTERPRETATION
AND HISTORY

1

Technique of
Dream Interpretation
and the Dreamwork

By the time he died his life had long been over, but at
death the whole past stirs within one.
I feel now as if I had been torn up by the roots.
Freud, to Wilhelm Fliess, November 2, 1896

Through the explication of some of the central
concepts in psycho-analytic theory, this section will show
how Freud's work creates possibilities for human freedom
within a specific genre of historical interpretation of psychological phenomena. The structure of Freud's approach to
dreams is the paradigm for all subsequent psycho-analytic
investigations and therefore will be of utmost importance here.
The particular approach to deciphering present signs by
means of their historical significations established in *The
Interpretation of Dreams* remains present throughout Freud's
work. This chapter will examine Freud's investigation of the
meaning of dreams and how that meaning is uncovered, the
mechanisms of the production of the dream's form, the
dreamwork, and the technique that "undoes" this production, interpretation. Freud's interpretive stance is most powerful when one regards psycho-analysis as a theory of history. The next three chapters will show that Freud's work is

first and foremost a theory of history aimed at establishing self-consciousness in the analysand. Dream interpretation, a key aspect of this theory, is an attempt to discover the development and meaning of the dream. Only when this discovery is accomplished can the significance of the dream be integrated into the person's understanding of the connections among his past, his present, and his desires.

In the summer of 1897 Sigmund Freud began his self-analysis, less than a year after the death of his father, and two years before the first chapters of *Die Traumdeutung (The Interpretation of Dreams)*, were sent to press.[1] This book was to be his magnum opus, the work that, as Freud would write in 1931, "contains . . . the most valuable of all the discoveries it has been my good fortune to make."[2] The theory of dream formation and interpretation was the major point of certainty for Freud throughout the years when psycho-analysis was developing, and the dream book would be one of two that he revised as psycho-analytic theory changed. "Whenever I began to have doubts of the correctness of my wavering conclusions," he noted near the end of his life, "the successful transformation of a senseless and muddled dream into a logical and intelligible mental process in the dreamer would renew my confidence of being on the right track."[3]

The Interpretation of Dreams was not Freud's first work, but rather marks a turning point in his thought; it is the start of psycho-analysis as a method and theory of interpretation rather than as an explanatory theory. The latter was an approach that characterized much of his work prior to his self-analysis, and the precision that his explanatory method seemed to require remained attractive to Freud throughout his life. However, even his most ambitious attempt to arrive at an explanatory theory of the mind, *The Project for a Scientific Psychology*, itself contains the seeds of the later in-

[1] Ernest Jones, *The Life and Work of Sigmund Freud*, vol. 1 (New York, 1953), 319–327.

[2] *The Interpretation of Dreams*, SE, IV, xxxii (preface to the third English edition).

[3] *New Introductory Lectures on Psycho-Analysis*, SE, XXII, 7.

terpretive method. As Paul Ricoeur notes, *The Project*'s use of a topographical anatomy rather than a physiological anatomy foreshadows the interpretive treatment used in the last chapter of the dream book.[4] The topographical approach to the mind makes use of a spatial metaphor to understand the meaning of the mind's functions, while the anatomical approach attempts directly to describe and to locate within the brain the processes that occur. Freud, as Ricoeur notes, consistently uses the former approach.

But what does Freud mean by "interpretation"? A good answer is found in Charcot's advice to him: "to look at the same things again and again until they themselves begin to speak."[5] The essential element in this description of interpretation is its emphasis on the *internal* nature of the process. That is, the meaning of the sign is not determined by something extraneous to it, but rather by the sign's position in relation to other signs and to the associations it generates. The meanings of the sign are fully grasped as a result of the process of seeing it in relation to the things (concepts, people, entities) that the sign itself *brings to mind*. At the same time, Freud seems to say that everything is a sign or, to put it another way, that everything has meaning, and that meanings can be understood only as the result of a process of interpretation. Understanding is not immediate, but is the result of a task. Interpretation is, then, as a preliminary definition, the process through which meaning is comprehended by the subject. The meaning of a thing takes into account its function, its relation to other things, and its immediate appearance.

Freud succinctly states the aim of the technique of dream interpretation in the opening paragraph of the second chapter of the *Interpretation of Dreams*: ". . . for 'interpreting' a dream implies assigning a 'meaning' to it—that is, replacing

---

[4]Paul Ricoeur, *Freud and Philosophy: An Essay on Interpretation*, trans. Denis Savage (New Haven, 1970), 84. Ricoeur notes that Freud in 1891 was already beginning to criticize theorists who were attempting to locate mental processes within the brain.

[5]Freud, *On the History of the Psycho-Analytic Movement*, SE, XIV, 22.

it by something which fits into the chain of our mental acts as a link having validity and importance equal to the rest."[6] By taking up this task of interpretation, Freud allies himself with the "lay world's" opinion of dreams inasmuch as both see the phenomenon as a psychical event and as meaningful. Although he recognizes that the popular belief about dreams is nearer to the truth than is scientific opinion, he is not blind to the limitations of the former. His project in *The Interpretation of Dreams* is to turn popular opinion into scientific knowledge by developing a systematic theoretical account of the genesis and significance of dreams.[7]

Freud turned his attention to dreams as a result of his work at unraveling *(Auflösung)* the symptoms of his neurotic patients. In this process the patients brought up their dreams as part of their associations with a "pathological idea." Freud explains: "It was then only a short step to treating the dream itself as a symptom and to applying to dreams the method of interpretation that had been worked out for symptoms."[8]

Treating the dream as a symptom is one of the primary conditions of the psycho-analytic approach. But what does Freud mean by "symptom"? In the *Introductory Lectures on Psycho-Analysis* he talks about the "sense of symptoms," their "whence" and their "whither." That is, he maintains that each symptom is made up of material from outside the subject (the "whence"), and that each has a purpose (the "whither"), which is an endopsychic process. Freud refers to the method of discovering this dual sense as the "historical interpretation of symptoms."[9]

The *O.E.D.* defines symptom, in part, as a "characteristic sign of some disease." Freud can be viewed as trying to determine what the sign signified and what the relationship between the sign and its source was. He concentrated on the

[6] *SE*, IV, 96.

[7] The issue of whether psycho-analysis is a science will not be directly addressed here. However, the nature of what Freud viewed as scientific, namely, interpretation, will be examined in detail.

[8] *The Interpretation of Dreams*, *SE*, IV, 101.

[9] *SE*, XVI, 284, 271.

process of signification, the process through which one thing came to signify another. In regard to dreams this process is called the dreamwork, and it has close affinities with the process of symptom formation. Most important, for both the process of signification is intelligible, meaningful.

Freud compares his attempt to find the meaning behind a dream with the method of interpretation used by the ancients. The differences between the two techniques, however, are most instructive. First, the ancients transposed the meaning of the dream into the future—made the meaning predictive. Second, the ancients, like the modern medical doctor, assigned meaning to the dream by means of a fixed key for translation. The relation between sign and signified was immediate, or rather, there was no relation at all except equivalence. That is not to say that in medicine the symptom has an immediately apparent univocal meaning, but once it is seen clearly it is in principle translatable. In medicine and in ancient interpretation the attempt is made to reach a meaning that is univocal. This attempt is not made in Freud's work.[10] In psycho-analysis the symptom is placed in a historical perspective, and the task of interpretation rests primarily on the bearer of the symptom. There is no fixed key or diagnostic manual that acts as a translator. As Freud says in regard to dreams: "The technique which I describe in the pages that follow differs in one essential respect from the ancient method: it imposes the task of interpretation upon the dreamer himself. It is not concerned with what occurs to the *interpreter* in connection with a particular element of the dream, but with what occurs to the *dreamer*."[11]

Calling the dream a symptom makes it the object of the unraveling; as symptom the dream is a phenomenon that has a meaning beyond the immediate one. The dream is a

---

[10] The problem of "typical dreams" and symbolism in dreams will be discussed in detail below, but the place Freud found for these factors in his overall theory and his repeated warnings about overestimating their importance are further indications of the absence of the search for a univocal meaning.

[11] *The Interpretation of Dreams*, SE, IV, 98.

characteristic sign of something else: of some pathological way of being. One must keep in mind here that Freud makes only quantitive distinctions between the normal and the abnormal, between health and disease. He certainly seems to say in *The Interpretation of Dreams* (especially in the last chapter) that the dream reveals a portion of ourselves that remains pathological, a portion of ourselves that has remained beyond our grasp.[12]

Besides the decision to treat the dream as a symptom, Freud sets two further preconditions for dream interpretation: the dreamer must pay attention to his own psychical perceptions, and he must eliminate the critical faculty through which he normally rejects certain of these perceptions.[13] These are the steps that *set the situation* for free association, or, as Freud sometimes puts it, the way in which involuntary ideas become voluntary.[14] The analysand attends to those ideas which "seem to emerge of their own free will," but does not exercise critical judgment upon them. He "follows" these thoughts and reports them to the analyst. Most important, he *keeps them in mind.* Freud quotes a letter of Schiller's: "Reason cannot form any opinion upon all this unless it retains the thought long enough to look at it in connection with others. On the other hand where there is a creative mind, Reason— so it seems to me—relaxes its watch upon the gates, and the ideas rush in pell-mell, and only then does it look them through and examine them in a mass."[15]

Keeping thoughts, which seem to arise spontaneously, in mind and reporting them to the analyst is the foundation of the technique of dream interpretation and of psycho-analysis generally. The name of this technique, "free association," actually describes four methods of dream interpretation that the analyst can use: *(a)* proceeding chronologically, by providing the analysand with stimuli for associations with the

[12] What Ricoeur, in *Freud and Philosophy*, calls "the Thing" that is in all of us.
[13] *The Interpretation of Dreams*, SE, IV, 101.
[14] Ibid., 102.
[15] Quoted in *The Interpretation of Dreams*, SE, IV, 103.

dream in the order that stimuli appeared in the account of the dream; *(b)* proceeding from a point in the report of the dream which stands out from the elements that surround it; *(c)* proceeding from the dreamer's associations with the events of the day just prior to the dream; *(d)* proceeding by allowing the dreamer to begin with any type of association he chooses. The "free" in free association, then, is modified by the direction provided by the analyst. Most important, the "free" refers to the relative absence of the critical faculty usually present in thought.[16]

What "free association" does not imply is that there are no principles governing the associations. The process of interpretation and association enables the analysand to discover the laws—which are described by the dreamwork—that underlie his associations. Finally, one can know the meaning of the interaction of the associations and the laws that govern them. Through the relative freedom of the associations, then, one arrives at the determinants of the dream, the *dream thoughts*.

The fundamental principle of psycho-analysis, that all things have meaning, is underscored here. There can be no arbitrary psychical events—all thoughts have a meaning that is fully understood only when they are seen in relation to their form (that is, whether they are unconscious, conscious, or dream thoughts) and to each other. "Whenever one psychical element is linked with another by an objectionable or superficial association," Freud noted, "there is also a legitimate and deeper link between them which is subjected to the resistance of the censorship."[17] This "deeper link" Freud described as an aim or a purpose ("purposive ideas"). In his investigation of neuroses as well as of dreams he always upheld the concept that all psychical events have some purpose for the person. It is through the concept of "purposive ideas" that the associations and the dream become compre-

---

[16] Freud, "Remarks on the Theory and Practice of Dream Interpretation," *SE*, xix, 109.

[17] *The Interpretation of Dreams*, *SE*, v, 530. This sentence is printed in bold type in the *Standard Edition*.

hensible. "For it is demonstrably untrue," he wrote, "that we are being carried along a purposeless stream of ideas when, in the process of interpreting a dream, we abandon reflection and allow involuntary ideas to emerge. It can be shown that all that we can ever get rid of are purposive ideas that are *known* to us."[18]

The unconscious purposive idea is the wish that is the instigator of the dream. Freud's theory that every dream represents the fulfillment of a wish is one of the central facets of the dream theory as a whole, but cannot be examined in detail here. What is relevant to this inquiry is that the discovery of the wish is the most important part of the interpretive process. Interpretation aims at discovering the origin or the stimulus of a dream. However, one must be sure to distinguish between the stimulus as a physiological occurrence and the stimulus as a mental event. Freud means the latter when he speaks of the wish, and although it is intimately connected with biological need, it should not be confused with it.

Here one gets to the core of the Freudian system of investigation. The psycho-analytic interpretation of dreams discovers the wish that is represented in the dream, but does not proceed beyond this discovery to discuss the physiological basis for the wish itself. To be sure, Freud enters into a complex metapsychological inquiry in the last chapter of *The Interpretation of Dreams*, but this is an investigation of the "frontier between the mental and the physical," not of the realm of the biologists (or even the neurologists). In this chapter Freud moves beyond the mental only inasmuch as he investigates laws that govern its operations and "systems" that operate according to these laws.

The pleasure-unpleasure principle is one of the two laws that determine mental functioning. Freud also refers to it as the "pleasure principle" and the "unpleasure principle." All three terms describe the tendency of an organism to achieve pleasure through the release of tension. (The "reality princi-

[18] Ibid., 528.

ple," the second law which determines mental functioning,
refers to the modifications made in the search for pleasure
by the conditions in the perceived world.) The release of tension is felt as pleasure, and the dream is an example of such
a release. The wish is the vehicle for the outlet of tensions; it
is the meaningful form in which the release is manifested.
Through the concept of "wish fulfillment" the pleasure principle is integrated into the purposive activity of the subject
as part of what the subject *desires*. This release—which others before Freud had seen as a purely physiological response
to the day's tension—is seen in *The Interpretation of Dreams*
as achieved through psychical events, through specific, purposive ideas that the subject by means of the technique of
free association makes voluntary or subject to his (conscious)
will.[19]

The psychical systems that Freud describes in chapter 7
of *The Interpretation of Dreams* are not physiological structures. He rejects the anatomical form of physiology in favor
of the topographial form of psychology: "I shall entirely dis-
regard the fact that the mental apparatus with which we are
here concerned is also known to us in the form of an anatomical preparation [*Präparat*], and I shall carefully avoid the
temptation to determine psychical locality in any anatomical
fashion. I shall remain upon psychological ground."[20] Freud
justifies the use of this form of inquiry as one would justify
any form of interpretation; by the insight it brings to the object of study: "Analogies of this kind are only intended to
assist us in our attempt to make the complications of mental
functioning intelligible by dissecting the function and assigning its different constituents to different component parts of
the apparatus."[21] Just as the "psychical systems" Freud discusses are the topographical form of what is often put in
anatomical terms, the "wish" that interpretation attempts to

---

[19] Freud speaks of involuntary ideas as having a "will of their own" in *The Interpretation of Dreams*, SE, ɪv, 102.
[20] *The Interpretation of Dreams*, SE, v, 536. "Preparation" can be read here as a presentation in a medical context.
[21] Ibid.

discover in the dream is the psychological form of the physiological pleasure principle.

Dream interpretation, then, revolves around four different types of free association that aim at discovering the "wish" within the dream. The process that leads backward to the wish—interpretation—is the reverse of the process through which the dream itself was formed. By isolating elements of the dream and tracing the associations of each of them so that the associations begin to have common elements, the dreamer arrives at the wish behind the dream and the unconscious thoughts that originally conveyed this wish. Once these dream thoughts are made conscious, they can be integrated, seen in relation to, the rest of the dreamer's thoughts, and their meaning can be established. The meaning of a dream is always found by the one who (re)experiences it, and the second stage of the process, judging the dream, can occur only when other material from the analysand's life is used. The dream, then, must be seen in relation to other efforts that the analysand has been making to find meaning and direction in his life.

A full understanding of the dream can come only with an investigation of the process that makes interpretation necessary, the dreamwork. The description of this process takes up over a third of *The Interpretation of Dreams.* Freud shows in this text the four major ways in which the latent dream thoughts are translated into the manifest content of the dream. The manifest dream signifies the dream thoughts, usually in a pictorial language. Interpretation translates these pictures back into thoughts that can be comprehended.

The dreamwork creates the form in which we are accustomed to experiencing dreams and is thus responsible for the difference between "night-thinking" and "waking-thinking." The question immediately arises as to why the form comes to exist as it does; what is its purpose?

The purpose of the form of dreams is found in two related concepts. The first, which has already been examined in some detail, is wish fulfillment. The form of the dream itself serves the wish to sleep, and this leads Freud to say that "dreams are the guardians of sleep." That is, the psychical energy that the dream thoughts carry with them would wake the person if these thoughts were to pass unmodified into consciousness. The form the thoughts take through the dreamwork allows one to remain asleep. The second concept that is central here is that of censorship or repression. The manifest content of the dream is a distorted form of the original dream thoughts. This distortion, besides serving the wish to sleep, also serves to prevent an understanding of the dream from occurring during waking life. In this way the energy of the psychical ideas is partially released, but their meaning—which would be threatening to the waking consciousness in that it would lead to conflict and tension—is kept separate from waking thought. The dreamwork has, then, both a positive and a negative purpose. On the one hand it creates a form that permits sleep to continue, and on the other hand it acts as a protector against ideas that would be too painful for the consciousness to bear undisguised.[22] In the language of the later topography: the dreamwork serves the ego, in the wish to sleep, and the id, in the release of prohibited unconscious thoughts, albeit in disguised form.[23]

The first element of the dreamwork that is discovered by the interpreter and discussed by Freud in the relevant texts is *condensation.* This process is evidenced by the "wealth" of the dream thoughts when seen in comparison with the "meager" content of the actual manifest dream. The fact that the manifest dream may represent only a fragment of the thoughts that lie behind it makes the interpretive process uncertain. There may always remain dream thoughts that have not yet been revealed by the associations. "Even if the solution seems satisfactory and without gaps," Freud noted, "the possibility always remains that the dream may have yet an-

[22] The idea that a person is made up of psychical things over which he does not have full control is crucial for Freud. It will be examined in detail below in Chapter 2. See also Donald Davidson, "Paradoxes of Irrationality," in *Philosophical Essays on Freud,* ed. Richard Wollheim and James Hopkins (Cambridge, 1982).

[23] See Freud, *New Introductory Lectures on Psycho-Analysis, SE,* xxii, 19.

other meaning. Strictly speaking, then, it is impossible to determine the amount of condensation."[24]

Through the process of condensation, many elements in
the latent dream thoughts become represented by a single
element in the manifest content "as though it were a combined allusion to all of them."[25] Figures in the manifest dream
are often composites of more than one person from waking
life, like the projection of many images onto a single photo-
graphic plate.[26] In this way one sees that the elements of the
manifest content are determined, in part, by many different
dream thoughts, since the latter are the instigators of the
dreamwork itself. For example, a figure in the experienced
dream may have the beard of the dreamer's uncle and the
name and other facial features of the dreamer's friend, and
one would regard the thoughts about the uncle and the friend
as the determinants of the figure in the dream.

The work of condensation leads to the concept of overdetermination. This term simply refers to the fact that the manifest dream element (or symptom, or any sign) has more than
one determinant. Interpretation must proceed from an identification of the determinants to the discovery of the relationships between them and their meanings. Freud comments
on the general nature of these relationships: "The direction
in which condensations in dreams proceed is determined on
the one hand by the rational preconscious relations of the
dream-thoughts, and on the other hand by the attraction ex-
ercised by visual memories in the unconscious. The outcome
of the activity of condensation is the achievement of the intensities required for forcing a way through the perceptual
systems."[27] The outcomes of condensation are often composite figures or compromise formations that act as a link
between two dream thoughts.[28] These formations are not
bound by the laws of logic or by common sense, but by the

[24] *The Interpretation of Dreams*, SE, IV, 279.
[25] Freud, *An Outline of Psycho-Analysis*, SE, XXIII, 168.
[26] An image Freud was fond of; see *SE*, IV, 293.
[27] *The Interpretation of Dreams*, SE, V, 596.
[28] Ibid.

intensities of the ideas involved. The re-report of the "Irma dream" in the section of *The Interpretation of Dreams* on condensation contains many examples of these compromise and composite figures. The manifest figure of Irma also represented: another patient of Freud's (through Irma's position standing at the window), Freud's daughter (through the diphtheritic membrane that Irma seemed to have), still another patient of Freud's (through the name of Freud's daughter and the associations with a patient who succumbed to poisoning), Freud's wife, and "another lady" (through Irma's recalcitrance over opening her mouth). The figure of Irma in this dream points to the ways in which the dream thoughts are distorted through condensation to endow a single figure with multiple meanings. Freud comments on this process:

> Thus a dream is not constructed by each individual dream-thought, or group of dream-thoughts, finding (in abbreviated form) separate representation in the content of the dream—in the kind of way in which an electorate chooses parliamentary representatives; a dream is constructed rather, by the whole mass of dream-thoughts being submitted to a sort of manipulative process in which those elements which have the most numerous and strongest supports acquire the right of entry into the dream-content in a manner analogous to election by *scrutin de liste*.[29]

Condensation results in the dream's multiple layers of meaning; the censorship is served by the apparently superficial association through which the composite figures are formed.[30]

[29] Ibid., *SE*, iv, 284.

[30] Roman Jakobson has offered an interesting suggestion on the linguistic characterization of the dreamwork. He views condensation as synecdochic, displacement as metonymic, and identification and symbolism—by which he means what I will call representation—as metaphoric. See "Two Aspects of Language and Two Types of Aphasic Disturbances," in Roman Jakobson and Morris Halle, *Fundamentals of Language* (2d. rev. ed., The Hague, 1971), 69–96. Linguistic and rhetorical approaches to the dreamwork, of which there are many, are attempts at uncovering the principles of signification through which latent dream thoughts are transposed into figures of the manifest dream. These approaches become especially valuable in light of

The second part of the dreamwork Freud describes is *dis-placement,* the *shifting of accent* from one dream element to another: "Thus something that played only a minor part in the dream-thoughts seems to be pushed into the foreground in the dream as the main thing, while, on the contrary, what was the essence of the dream-thoughts finds only passing and indirect representation in the dream."[31] This shifting of accent takes place in two ways: a dream thought is replaced by an allusion to something else, and the psychical intensity of one idea is shifted to another. The allusions that are created by displacement are often superficial or remote and have little to do with the central meaning of that which is being represented or with the "representer." These allusions are similar to the ones found in jokes, being based on phonological similarity, contiguity in space, or simultaneity in time. The dream allusion differs from the kind used in jokes, however, in that the dream's associations are "strained," hard to follow. Freud saw the purpose of these allusions as being to serve the censorship. Indeed, he identified displacement as the "principal means of dream distortion."[32] Condensation plays less of a role in distortion than displacement, since this latter process is more likely to make use of external associations; for example, the patient is represented by another per-

---

the work of Lacan, who sees the unconscious as structured like a language. For some useful summaries of Lacan, see David James Fisher, "Lacan's Ambiguous Impact on Contemporary French Psychoanalysis," *Contemporary French Civilization,* 6 (Fall/Winter 1981–1982), 89–114, and the symposium on Lacan in the *Psychoanalytic Review,* 69 (1982). See also: *Returning to Freud: Clinical Psychoanalysis in the School of Lacan,* ed. and trans. Stuart Schneiderman (New Haven, 1980); Jane Gallop, *The Daughter's Seduction: Feminism and Psychoanalysis* (Ithaca, 1984), and *Reading Lacan* (Ithaca, 1985). See also the provocative critique in Luc Ferry and Alain Renault, *La pensée 68* (Paris, 1985), chap. 6. The literature on Lacan is growing steadily, and these citations merely scratch the surface of it.

[31] *New Introductory Lectures on Psycho-Analysis, SE,* xxii, 21.

[32] Ibid. See also the discussion of displacement in *Jokes and Their Relation to the Unconscious, SE,* viii, keeping in mind that dreams use displacements "like a bad joke." On the importance of jokes to the development of Freud's theoretical stance, see Samuel Weber, *The Legend of Freud* (Minneapolis, 1982), 84–87.

son's position by the window in condensation, while displacement might merely show a window to represent the
patient.

The third element of the dreamwork is the transformation
of thoughts into images, or *representation*. This process adds
to the confusing nature of the dream experience because of
the great difficulty involved in transforming certain thoughts
in this way. This is especially the case with thoughts that
express logical relations such as the concepts "therefore" and
"because." For this reason causality is often represented by
a temporal sequence of pictures, and the possibility of alter-
natives, a sense of "either-or," is not to be found in dreams
at all. Contradiction, Freud says, is entirely disregarded in
dreams.[33]

Freud draws one of the keys to understanding the process
of representation in dreams from the history of language. He
sees the dream as a kind of primitive language and points to
similarities between it and early speech. However, the major
difference between the dream and any type of language is
crucial. The latter is usually an attempt to communicate, to
be understood; the former is always an attempt to block understanding. Nonetheless, the importance of the comparison
should not be overlooked. The workings of the dream are
closely tied to the workings of language, to the general principles of signification, and this is an invaluable aid to the
interpreter: "In the case of symbolic dream-interpretation the
key to the symbolization is arbitrarily chosen by the interpreter; whereas in our cases of verbal disguise the keys are
generally known and laid down by firmly established linguistic usage."[34]

"Firmly established linguistic usage" is perhaps the most
important guide that the interpreter has in his attempt to see
through the distortion of the censorship. It is also the key in
the treatment of the neuroses, the symptoms of which are
formed according to the same patterns as are the dream's

[33] *The Interpretation of Dreams, SE*, ɪv, 318.
[34] Ibid., *SE*, v, 341–342.

elements. Interpretation is based upon the attempt to reverse this process, to translate these expressions which disguise communication into a content that is meaningful—that
can be integrated into the rest of our significations. "Whenever neuroses make use of such disguises," Freud writes, "they
are following paths along which all humanity passed in the
earliest periods of civilization—paths of whose continued existence today, under the thinnest of veils, evidence is to be
found in linguistic usages, superstitions and customs."[35]

The work of representation in dreams leads into another
area of dream formation that is not part of the dreamwork
as such, but is no less important. This is the repeated occurrence of symbols in dreams. Freud did not consider the
dreamwork to have symbolization as an inherent feature (although a discussion of symbolization is found in chapter 6
of *The Interpretation of Dreams*, which is entitled "The Dream-
Work"), but he did think that it "had access to the use of
symbols." He took some time to realize the full importance
of symbols in dreams, and in 1914 an entire section on the
subject was added to *The Interpretation of Dreams*.[36] The
presence of symbols in dreams makes interpretation possible
without the use of the dreamer's associations. The symbols
found in dreams are *directly translatable*, and they are also
found in myths, religions, arts, and language.[37]

The technique of interpretation in psycho-analysis is carried out essentially by the dreamer. With the increased importance of symbols—symbols being translatable by the analyst according to a fixed key—the major difference between
psycho-analytic and other forms of dream interpretation
seemed to disappear. Freud was certainly aware of this fact
and guarded carefully against the notion that the importance
of symbols reduced the importance of the standard psycho-
analytic technique in any way. He is clear on this point:

[35] Ibid., 347.

[36] Ibid., *SE*, IV, xviii (editor's introduction).

[37] Freud also notes that the symbols used in dreams are almost always
limited to representing sexual thoughts. See *Introductory Lectures on Psycho-Analysis*, *SE*, xv, 153.

"Interpretation based on a knowledge of symbols is not a technique which can replace or compete with the associative one. It forms a supplement to the latter and yields results which are only of use when introduced into it."[38] The immediate meaning of symbols, although important and fascinating, became relevant to the dreamer only because of its relationship with his other associations with the dream. Symbolic translation remains subordinate to the interpretation by the dreamer.

Through the associations one can see the origins of the various elements employed by the dreamwork in experience and imagination. However, the presence of symbols in dreams often occurred without the dreamer having any "knowledge" of them at all. What could be the origin of these apparently universal images? Although this question cannot be explored in detail here, it is important to note that Freud once again turns to the history of language for support.[39] Although his discussion of the work of the philologist Hans Sperber is not meant to be conclusive, Freud does place some importance on the connections between the sexual basis of language and sexual symbolism in dreams.[40]

The fourth and final facet of the dreamwork proper is the *secondary revision*.[41] This process takes place as the dream is being presented to consciousness. It "fills in the gaps," "makes connections," so that the dream appears as a whole, possibly even a coherent whole. Despite the coherence, Freud sees the secondary revision as primarily serving the purpose of the censorship: "Dreams which are of such a kind [logical dreams] have been subjected to a far-reaching revision by this psychical function that is akin to waking thought; they

[38] Ibid., 151. On the importance of symbolism in Freud's dream theory, see John Forrester, *Language and the Origins of Psychoanalysis* (New York, 1980), 70–76.

[39] Ibid., 165–169.

[40] Ibid., 167.

[41] Strachey notes that in two texts, an encyclopedia article and in "An Evidential Dream" (1913a), secondary revision is excluded from the dreamwork. Freud usually included it, however, and it is seen as part of the dreamwork in this essay.

49

appear to have a meaning, but that meaning is far removed as possible from their true significance."[42]

The most important implication of the process of secondary revision is that the censorship actually adds to the content of the dream in order to distort it. For example, the appearance of the thought, "Well, this is only a dream," within the dream experience Freud took to be direct evidence of the presence of the censor within the dream in order to *demean* it. "There can be no doubt," he wrote, "that the censoring agency, whose influence we have so far only recognized in limitations and omissions in the dream-content, is also responsible for interpolations and additions in it."[43] These additions do not mean that the dreamwork is creative. The feelings that the secondary revision makes use of are contained in the latent dream thoughts, perhaps in another context. If the dreamwork itself had created these feelings, then they could be dismissed as irrelevant to us in our waking hours. However, since the latent dream thoughts are the same as thoughts one has when one is awake, they cannot be dismissed as "merely belonging to the realm of sleep." The dreamwork merely makes use of—distorts—these thoughts.

The discussions of both the technique of dream interpretation and the dreamwork reveal not the effort to ground the sense of a dream in an explanation of its origins, but rather a consistent effort to decipher signs that express, but also block and disguise, the meanings and directions of a past. Freud's technique of free association, the crux of dream interpretation,[44] was shown to be a process through which one can achieve an understanding of part of oneself that previously seemed to have "a will of its own." By examining the psycho-analytic study of neurosis we shall see that this un-

---

[42] *The Interpretation of Dreams*, SE, v, 490.

[43] Ibid., 489.

[44] Free association is at least the crux of the first part of dream interpretation, translating the dream. The second part of the process, judging the dream, was not discussed at length here because it involves many other facets of the analysis not directly connected with the dream theory.

derstanding is the first step toward the integration of this part of oneself with the rest of one's conscious identity.

The technique of dream interpretation can be fully understood only when one undertakes an inquiry into its opposite, the dreamwork. My investigation of the relevant texts showed that Freud consistently made connections between his theory of dream formation and linguistic usage or history of language. Both structures—dreams and language—seemed to be conditioned in similar ways, and progress in the study of each phenomenon should prove useful for the other inquiry. Language theory can provide psycho-analysis with principles of signification which lend insight into the workings of the unconscious, and psycho-analysis can show the individual, unconscious, basis for particular transformations in language.

The inquiry into Freud's theory of the dreamwork also showed that psycho-analysis remained limited to the domain of the mental in dream theory. That is, psycho-analysis investigated a psychical occurrence, dreams, on a purely psychical level, and was able to derive meaning through interpretation without recourse to a "biological bedrock." This inability of interpretation to be truly completed, coupled with Freud's claim that the process arrives at points of significant meaning, confronts the reader with what has been called the "Freudian hermeneutics"—a form of investigation characteristic of his entire corpus.

In summary, it seems clear that, for Freud, showing how an action emerged out of a past coincided with showing that that activity was meaningful. It will become clear that Freud regarded the acknowledging of this meaning as the precondition for the achievement of any sort of freedom.

2

Repression

> Thus we obtain our concept of the unconscious from
> the theory of repression. The repressed is the proto-
> type of the unconscious for us.
>
> Freud, *The Ego and the Id*

> No substitutive or reactive formations and no sublima-
> tions will suffice to remove the repressed instinct's per-
> sisting tension.
>
> Freud, *Beyond the Pleasure Principle*

The investigation of Freud's theory of repression is
complicated by a host of difficulties. Unlike the theory of
dreams, expounded in *The Interpretation of Dreams*, and the
theory of infantile sexuality, treated in *Three Essays on the
Theory of Sexuality*, the subject is not dealt with in any one
major text. There is, however, no shortage of discussions of
repression in Freud's corpus; one may safely say that repression plays a crucial role in all his major works.

Our examination of the dream theory—specifically, the
technique of dream interpretation and the dreamwork—underscored the importance of "voluntary and involuntary ideas,"
the process of transformation and what was referred to as
the "release of tension," and the relationship of the dream as
a pathological structure to normal thought. All three of these
facets of the dream theory are also central in Freud's conception of repression. In this chapter I will examine repression in connection with all three. Voluntary and involuntary

ideas will be considered in terms of what Freud called the phenomenon of "knowing yet not knowing"; the process of transformation will be approached via a study of Freud's "Repression" (1915), and *Inhibitions, Symptoms, and Anxiety* (1926); and the relationship of pathology to what is "normal" will be looked at in terms of Freud's discussion of the results of repression.

In the theory of dreams, involuntary ideas were described as thoughts which "seem to emerge of their own free will." The goal of free association, as was emphasized above, was to make these involuntary ideas voluntary, to integrate them with the rest of our thoughts through understanding them. The origin of these intruding thoughts, though, was left more or less unexplained. They could be regarded as part of the latent dream content, but this explanation is not fully satisfactory, since it is clear that these ideas arise in contexts other than dream interpretation. Besides the problem of the origin of these involuntary thoughts, there also remains the important question of what purpose they serve outside of dreams. The facet of the theory of repression that deals with the phenomenon of "knowing yet not knowing" helps to fill the gaps in the concept of voluntary and involuntary ideas.

One of the first descriptions of the phenomenon of knowing yet not knowing—of the "presence" of involuntary ideas— is found in a case history in which Freud makes no mention of dream interpretation. He comes upon the phenomenon when he is questioning a patient, Miss Lucy R., about what he believes to be a rather sensitive subject:

> "I believe that really you are in love with your employer, the Director, though perhaps without being aware of it yourself. . . ." She answered in her usual laconic fashion: "Yes, I think that's true"—"But if you knew you loved your employer why didn't you tell me?"—"I didn't know—or rather I didn't want to know. I wanted to drive it out of my head and not think of it again; and I believe latterly I have succeeded."

Freud adds in a footnote to this passage: "I have never managed to give a better description of that strange state of mind

53

in which one knows and does not know a thing at the same time."[1]

This attempt to "drive it [the thought] out of my head" is similar but not identical to repression. The patient here is aware of not wanting to know something and intentionally tries to keep it out of mind. "Repression," as we shall see, usually implies that the person is not aware of not wanting to know—*it is an unconscious process.* Even though Freud, in *Studies on Hysteria* (1895), continues to talk about thoughts the person did not wish to know as being repressed, and even uses the term "intentionally repressed,"[2] this wish or intent seems to be present in the person only initially, and it quickly becomes clear to the analyst that the person is not just unaware of his desire not to know, but forcefully refuses to acknowledge the presence of this desire when informed about it. Freud describes this refusal, noting that since his insistence that a certain desire existed in the person "involved effort on my part and so suggested the idea that I had to overcome a resistance, the situation led me to the theory that *by means of my psychical work I had to overcome a psychical force in the patients which was opposed to the pathogenic ideas becoming conscious (being remembered)*."[3] This psychical force is repression, and the descriptions of it in *Studies on Hysteria* were to remain, in Freud's view, fundamentally accurate.

As psycho-analysis developed, the evidence of the phenomenon of knowing yet not knowing and the theoretical work done on the subject increased tremendously. In the dream theory numerous descriptions of the phenomenon appear; indeed, the forgetting of dreams is almost prototypical of the ways in which the analysand displays the usual absence of particular ideas that he is at certain moments aware of. Freud sees this forgetting as serving the purpose of the

[1] "Miss Lucy R.," from Freud and Joseph Breuer, *Studies on Hysteria*, SE, II, 117. I am indebted to Robert Steele for calling my attention to this passage.

[2] Ibid., 10, 123.

[3] Ibid., 69. The emphasis is in the original.

54

censorship: "Previous writers have had less justification in devoting so much space to the *doubt* with which our judgement receives accounts of dreams. For this doubt has no intellectual warrant. . . . Doubt whether a dream or certain of its details have been correctly reported is once more a derivation of the dream censorship, of resistance to the penetration of the dream-thoughts into consciousness."[4] The image of the "censorship," which Freud makes use of throughout his writings to describe the dynamic divisions in consciousness, reflects both the heuristic power of the concept of a "split mind" and the difficulties inherent in such a notion. These must be explored, since this concept—as the basis for the unconscious-conscious division as well as later topographies—is fundamental for psycho-analysis; most, if not all, of Freud's insights depend upon it. The phenomenon of knowing yet not knowing makes the theoretical development of a division of consciousness a necessity.

Freud made use of the notion of a divided consciousness early in his work.[5] In 1895 he described the process through which an idea is pushed back into unconsciousness as follows: "That idea is not annihilated by a repudiation of this kind, but merely repressed into the unconscious. When this process occurs for the first time there comes into being a nucleus and center of crystallization for the formation of a psychical group divorced from the ego."[6] A more descriptive passage, published thirty-eight years later, supplements the earlier one: "If we throw a crystal to the floor, it breaks; but not into haphazard pieces. It comes apart along its lines of cleavage into fragments whose boundaries, though they were invisible, were predetermined by the crystal's structure. Mental patients are split and broken structures of the same kind."[7] This division of the psyche into intersecting parts accounts

---

[4] *The Interpretation of Dreams*, SE, v, 513.

[5] The concept is usually, and rightly, seen in terms of the division of the psyche into unconscious, preconscious, conscious or, in the later topography, id, ego, and superego. The two divisions are not parallel.

[6] *Studies on Hysteria*, SE, ii, 123.

[7] *New Introductory Lectures on Psycho-Analysis*, SE, xxii, 59.

for the fact that one can "know yet not know." One can rightly say that the unified "I" as subject was denied by Freud. More accurately, this unified "I" was seen as something to be aimed at, not something given; the integration of the "involuntary" facets of one's personality into knowing is the progress toward the "I" as subject. It is a "progress" that is never complete. I pointed to this process of integration in the discussion of the dream theory above—the technique of dream interpretation aimed at making the dream thoughts meaningful to the analysand by undoing the distortion which they had undergone. In short, the technique aimed at integrating "night-thinking" with "day-thinking."

This view that Freud rejects a unified consciousness has often led to serious misunderstandings of psycho-analysis by both layman and scholars. Although the processes of the unconscious may be as foreign to us as the processes of other minds, Freud does not imply that the unconscious should be regarded as something beyond ourselves, something we are not responsible for. Although the ideas that spring from the unconscious seem to have "a will of their own," they are in fact very much part of us. Freud is emphatic on this point:

> Obviously one must hold oneself responsible for the evil impulses of one's dreams. What else is one to do with them? Unless the content of the dream (rightly understood) is inspired by alien spirits, it is a part of my own being. If I seek to classify the impulses that are present within me according to social standards into good and bad, I must assume responsibility for both sorts; and if, in defence, I say that what is unknown, unconscious and repressed in me is not my "ego," then I shall not be basing my position on psycho-analysis, I shall not have accepted its conclusions—and I shall perhaps be taught better by the criticisms of my fellowmen, by the disturbances in my actions and the confusion of my feelings. I shall perhaps learn that what I am disavowing not only "is" in me but "acts" from out of me as well.[8]

---

[8] "Some Additional Notes on Dream Interpretation as a Whole," *SE*, xix, 133.

Freud's theory of the mind, then, does not merely destroy the unity of the "I." Rather, it extends the possibilities for this unity by making it the goal of a task. The subject's psychology is made up of all the facets of his mind; his actions are the result of the dynamic relations among them. The responsibility of the "I" is not merely the responsibility for those facets of the mind "with which we are most familiar"—the ego, the conscious; the attempt must be made to grasp and know the processes that run beneath these structures.

The agency that operates between the structures of the mind is, as we know from the examination of dream theory, the censorship. This agency functions to keep painful ideas of certain kinds outside of consciousness or to distort these ideas to such an extent that they are no longer painful to us. Freud uses as a metaphor for the censorship the image of the entrance to a drawing room where a guard pushes back those people who are unfit to enter.[9] This pushing back is a repression from the "preconscious" (Freud's term for a facet of the mind which contains thoughts that are not conscious at that particular moment but could be without any real effort) to the unconscious.

Jean-Paul Sartre's criticism of the notion of the censorship, and of the unconscious generally, although based on a misunderstanding of Freud's work, clarifies some of the issues in the phenomenon of knowing yet not knowing. "But what type of self-consciousness can the censor have?" he asked. "It must be the consciousness (of) being conscious of the drive to be repressed, but precisely in order not to be conscious of it. What does this mean if not that the censor is in bad faith?" Sartre points out that the censorship must know what it is not allowed to know and that psycho-analysis "reifies bad faith," or gives a natural status to a chosen immoral act.[10] The censor does indeed have to be aware of those ideas which must be "pushed out of mind." The system of a di-

[9] See *Introductory Lectures on Psycho-Analysis*, SE, xvi, 295–296. See also *Five Lectures on Psycho-Analysis*, SE, xi, 25–27.

[10] Sartre, "*Mauvaise Foi* and the Unconscious," in *Freud: A Collection of Critical Essays*, ed. Richard Wollheim (Garden City, N.Y., 1974), 77.

vided consciousness explains this phenomenon as "knowing yet not knowing." Sartre's criticism is based upon the idea that there is an evasion of responsibility going one here; that one confronts oneself as an Other without having to be fully honest, since the Other in oneself can be doing the lying. If the Other tells the lie or is in bad faith, then no one is in bad faith; at least the "I" is not. It was shown above, however, that this evasion of responsibility—this reestablishment of the "I" through a denial of the parts of oneself that one does not want to recognize as parts of oneself, and the claim that they are part of an Other that just happens to be within the "I"— is explicitly rejected by Freud as something foreign to psycho-analytic findings. Rather than reifying bad faith, Freud's work provides a theory of interpretation that allows one to recognize the frequency of the occurrence of bad faith. The analysis of the formation and activity of the superego (the heir to the censorship) in his later work shows in detail the basis for the censorship in the concepts of introjection and identification with the father. By revealing this basis, psychoanalysis creates the possibility for a consciousness that would not deny its own meaning.[11]

The post-structuralist critique of Freud takes an entirely different tack from Sartre's and is worth mentioning here.[12] Rather than attacking Freud for dividing consciousness and thus permitting a reification of immorality, this criticism calls into question Freud's making the unity of the "I" the goal of a task. Freud should be applauded for recognizing that our

[11] For a discussion of some of the major criticisms of Freud's notion of the divided consciousness, see Gabriel Yiannis, "The Fate of the Unconscious in the Human Sciences," *Psychoanalytic Quarterly*, 51 (1981), 246–283. For a defense of Freud in this regard, see Donald Davidson, "Paradoxes of Irrationality," in *Philosophical Essays on Freud*, ed. Richard Wollheim and James Hopkins (Cambridge, 1982).

[12] Included in the category thus vaguely identified would be some of the criticisms of Freud and psychoanalysis made by Foucault, Derrida, and especially Deleuze. In this regard, see also Paul Ricoeur, *Freud and Philosophy: An Essay on Interpretation* (New Haven, 1970), chap. 2, especially 419–430; and Samuel Weber, *The Legend of Freud* (Minneapolis, 1982), 121–126, 129–130.

cogito cannot function as a foundation for our being in the world, but he should be rejected insofar as he still longs for an integrated self, or what Gilles Deleuze has called a "transcendental ground."[13]

This contemporary criticism of Freud belongs to the postmodern celebration of discontinuity and heterogeneity. Freud occupies a strange place in "the postmodern" since he recognizes these aspects of our lives without celebrating them. Although psycho-analysis as a theory of history in no way presupposes continuity in development (on the contrary, it underlines traumatic breaks in development), it does attempt to make meaning out of memory and rejects the Nietzschean forgetting and playful repetition so dear to many contemporary French critics and their American followers.

But it should be underlined that for Freud the "divided consciousness" is not something that can be overcome through analysis or anything else in life. Instead, the "I" as subject is never unified, and never a stable foundation for our action or our intellection. This divided consciousness, slippery slope though it may be, is that from (and through) which we give meaning and direction to our lives. The fact that we have no more stable foundation for making sense of ourselves in the world is an occasion neither for play nor for despair in psycho-analysis. It is simply the condition that we must apprehend as we come to acknowledge the past in the service of the present.

The discovery of the universality of something like the neurotic knowing yet not knowing is made possible by the theoretical development of structures of the mind that can account for this abnormal phenomenon. The presupposition here—and it underlies the whole of psycho-analytic theory— is that the abnormal is merely an exaggerated form of the normal. As the number and variety of the cases of this phenomenon grew, Freud attempted to develop a more precise

[13] See, for example, Deleuze, *Presentation de Sacher-Masoch* (Paris, 1967), 114.

and general account of repression, "the force that kept one from knowing." The investigation of knowing yet not knowing, starting at least as early as 1895 in *Studies on Hysteria,* along with the analysis of voluntary and involuntary ideas highlighted in 1900 in *The Interpretation of Dreams,* made a systematic account of the process of repression a necessity for psycho-analytic theory. The first such account is found in "Repression," one of the *Papers on Metapsychology* (1915), and the second in *Inhibitions, Symptoms, and Anxiety* (1926). An explication of the descriptions of the dynamic, economic, and topographical perspectives that these works contain will clarify Freud's conception of the mechanism as a transformation and release of tension. Such an explication lays the groundwork for some comments on the role of the concept of repression in the relationship between the abnormal and the normal.

The essay "Repression" contains the most detailed description of the mechanism to be found in Freud's corpus. It was published at a time when his ideas were going through some fundamental revisions, and can be regarded as an attempt to reaffirm some of the basic conclusions of psycho-analysis by reworking the theory of this key process. Although it is not appropriate to place this essay in a full historical perspective here, some events just prior to its publication need to be mentioned. In 1913 Carl Jung and Freud formally broke off relations with each other, and the break arose in part over the place of sexuality as an unconscious force. The problems that Jung raised in regard to the place of sexuality in human psychology were responded to, again only in part, by Freud's 1914 essay "On Narcissism: An Introduction."[14] This essay marks a transition point in the history of psycho-analysis; it offers a new picture of the ego-libido relationship in which the ego has access to the unconscious domain of sexuality.

By tying the ego so closely to sexuality in "On Narcissism," Freud was reversing an earlier part of the theory which viewed libido (most easily understood as energy that underlies the

[14]*SE,* xiv, 67–102.

sexual instinct),[15] as a "force dreaded by the ego and com-
bated by means of repression."[16] In "On Narcissism" the libidinal and ego instincts are described as being "inseparably
mingled," and acting in harmony with each other.[17] That essay establishes the great importance of the ego by giving it a
dual function: on the one hand it acts as a "prohibitor" and
battles the forces of sexuality, and on the other hand it acts
as an object of desire and draws the libido to itself.[18] However, it is by no means clear how this conception of a "new
ego" fits in with the rest of the theory. In "Repression," Freud
is trying to come to grips with the problems raised by Jung's
work and the essay on narcissism, as well as trying to offer a
conclusive summary of the relevant theory.[19]

Repression, Freud tells the reader at the start of the essay,
is a middle ground between the mechanism of flight from a
feared external object and the condemnation of an impulse
that one does not want to act upon.[20] The ego cannot, of
course, flee from the impulses that arise within the person,
and the conscious condemnation of an instinctual force occurs only when the person has reached a level of maturity at
which he can consider the impulses his own and work them
through. The concept of repression presupposes a *topographical division* of the mind—that is, a division of the mind
based on a figurative representation of parts of the psyche
by means of a spatial metaphor. The topography that Freud

---

[15] For this definition, and many others given in this essay, see J. Laplanche and J.-B. Pontalis, *The Language of Psycho-Analysis*, trans. Donald
Nicholson-Smith (New York, 1973).

[16] *The Interpretation of Dreams*, SE, v, 410.

[17] *SE*, xiv, 92.

[18] It would be difficult to overestimate the importance of the essay on
narcissism for the subsequent development of psycho-analysis. Besides re-
defining the role of the ego, it is crucial for the evolution of instinct theory,
the later investigations into femininity and the acquisition of sexual identity, the theoretical understanding of the superego, and important elements
in the mechanisms of mourning.

[19] One of the reasons for this attempt at a conclusive summary seems to
be Freud's belief that he was going to die in 1918. See Jones, *The Life and
Work of Sigmund Freud*, vol. ii (New York, 1955), 194

[20] "Repression," *SE*, xiv, 146.

61

was using in 1915 was Conscious, Preconscious, and Unconscious, and repression was seen in terms of the conflict between these parts. Freud describes the conflict:

> Psycho-analytic observation of the transference neuroses, moreover, leads us to conclude that repression is not a defensive mechanism which is present from the very beginning, and that it cannot arise until a sharp cleavage has occurred between conscious and unconscious mental activity—that *the essence of repression lies simply in turning something away, and keeping it at a distance, from the conscious.*[21]

This turning the impulse away is the subject's attempt to escape from his ambivalence—the conflict of opposing desires. In repression, the subject "chooses" to act in accordance with one of his desires, but it is a choice that is made unaware of the conflict which presupposes it.

The first problem that arises with this descriptive account of repression, Freud says, is in the meaning of "ambivalence." It seems paradoxical that the instinct is denied release by repression since release is felt as pleasure by the subject. The ego dreads the satisfaction of some impulses, so it actively prevents their release. The pleasure principle seems, then, to be overturned during this process, and one is tempted to talk about the reality principle, or some kind of "social pressure." Such reasoning, however, would not be entirely accurate. An impulse is repressed because its satisfaction would lead to the arousal of other desires that would result in further conflict for the subject. Such conflicts would result in a serious inability to act, and hence to a buildup of tension and pain. This dynamic of repression to avoid conflict is especially clear when one considers that the impulse repressed by the adult is often infantile in character. Freud notes that the satisfaction of an instinct "would, therefore, cause pleasure in one place and unpleasure in another. It has consequently become a condition for repression that the

---

[21] Ibid., 147.

motive force of unpleasure shall have acquired more strength than the pleasure obtained from satisfaction."[22]

It is evident that the description of repression as turning an impulse away—making a choice without knowledge of the options that exist—places a premium on the phenomenon of knowing yet not knowing. The question now arises how one can know what the analysand knows, and how the subject can turn away an impulse that he does not know about. What is crucial here is that the analysand does not communicate a conscious knowledge of the impulse to the analyst. The knowledge is absent—in the strong senses of the words, it is "visibly missing"—from the manifest discourse between the two. But, it is also present in the latent discourse and is evidenced by the particular manifestations, signs, that the analysand makes use of. The question whether the analysand "really knows" of the impulse is irrelevant to psychoanalysis. Through interpretation, the impulse's function in the analysand's discourse can be discovered; the object of interpretation is this discourse, not any "real knowledge" that his words may conceal. Such a concealment would be meaningful as part of the analysand's discourse itself but would not deny the validity of interpretation.

On a general level, then, the description of repression as the "turning away" of an impulse stands firm. Freud goes on (in "Repression") to distinguish between two phases, *primal repression* and *repression proper*. The former refers to the initial stage at which the ideational representative of a drive is denied access into consciousness and becomes fixated to the energy of the drive. In other words, the representative idea retains a certain potency as a result of having been initially joined with an instinct. This potency is described by Freud as the "quota of affect." "Primal repression" is important since it offers an explanation of the peculiar way in which infantile wishes reappear in adult life.[23] It is through the fix-

[22]Ibid.
[23]Jonathan Cohen and Warren Kingston emphasize that primal repression can occur at any stage in life, not just in childhood, in "Repression Theory," *IJP*, 65 (1984), 411–422.

ation of an idea and a drive at an early age that a particular object can remain an important vehicle for sexual satisfaction in later life. The sexual drive and its representative remain active in the unconscious and do not die away as changes in the external life of the person take place. Commenting on the active existence of the past in the unconscious, Freud says that psycho-analysis "shows us, for instance, that the instinctual representative develops with less interference and more profusely if it is withdrawn by repression from conscious influence. It proliferates in the dark, as it were, and takes on extreme forms of expression."[24]

Such proliferation leads to the second stage of repression, "repression proper." This mechanism is concerned with the derivatives of the original representation that was repressed—thoughts that have become connected with it through paths of association much the same as those in the dreamwork. Repression proper has, then, two important facets to its operation: the attraction of that which is originally repressed for ideas which are also in the unconscious and can be connected with it through association; and the force against these associations which keeps them from becoming conscious (Freud sometimes referred to this as "after-pressure," or "after-repression").

The dream is itself an example of a structure that has been affected by repression proper. It appears only during "sleeping-consciousness," and then only in a highly distorted form. The appearance of the dream is important because it shows the limitations of repression as a mechanism for the protection of the ego. The unconscious representative finds some form of release through the use of the distortion of the dreamwork; its expression in the manifest dream is one of the ways the existence of the representative can be discovered. If the repressed impulse remained in the unconscious we would have no reason to bother about it; indeed, we would never have any indication that it exists. The only way in which we become aware of its existence (the "knowing" in "know-

[24] "Repression," *SE*, xiv, 149.

ing yet not knowing") is through the appearance of these associated signs—thoughts, dreams, symptoms of neurosis. The further in meaning the association is from the original repressed idea, the more likely is the association to enter the conscious. "If these derivatives have become sufficiently far removed from the repressed representative," Freud notes, "whether owing to the adoption of distortions or by reason of the number of intermediate links inserted, they have free access to the conscious. It is as though the resistance of the conscious against them was a function of their distance from what was originally repressed."[25]

This process of association and after-pressure is part of the dynamic facet of repression. The dynamic facet is one of conflict and the attempted resolution of (or escape from) conflict. Repression proper involves what Freud called "a delicate balancing," and the process acts in "a highly individual manner."[26] Whether a thought will be admitted to consciousness may depend on a slight degree of distortion. With a certain disguise the thought (or the impulse behind the thought) would appear very appealing; without it the thought would arouse great disgust. Freud says: "In this connection we can understand how it is that the objects to which men give most preference, their ideals, proceed from the same perceptions and experiences as the objects they most abhor, and that they were originally only distinguished from one another through slight modifications."[27]

The way in which the multifarious associations of the representative attempt to enter the conscious leads Freud to conclude that the expenditure of energy required by repression must be constant. In order to ensure that associations that have a close connection with the original representative do not penetrate consciousness, the ego must turn a portion of its energies toward the internal realm. In the state of sleep this attention is somewhat relaxed, and dreaming can take place. This economic aspect of repression—the fact that the

[25] Ibid.
[26] Ibid., 150.
[27] Ibid.

ego has a fixed store of energy—is central for the way in which psycho-analysis defines its therapeutic task. That is, the expenditure of energy by the ego to guard against the internal realm limits its ability to act in the world. By lifting a repression the analyst frees this energy for action. That is not to say that the psycho-analyst aims at seeing the repressed impulse receive gratification, but he does want to see it enter consciousness so that the analysand is aware of its existence. Through the process of repression the analysand takes one course of action rather than another—follows one impulse without understanding its development and relationships to his other thoughts and feelings. After the removal of a repression the analysand can choose because he can acknowledge his conflicting desires. The demands on ego energy made by repression, as well as the fact that repression is a turning away from a part of oneself from which one cannot flee and which will not decay, make its removal a liberating experience. It is a liberation from a blindness to a part of one's history; a liberation to channel the energy, used previously to maintain this blindness, into action in the present.

The internal workings of the mechanism of repression are known to us only through the outcome of the process. This outcome is actually evidence of a failure of repression. An example of such evidence is, of course, dreams, which have been discussed at some length as examples of the relaxing of repression. The major evidence of repression with which psycho-analysis deals is the symptoms of the neuroses. In anxiety hysteria, particularly in animal phobias, the process is "completely unsuccessful" since the affect of the original representative is transformed into an anxiety, and the idea that was feared is displaced, through associations, to an external object.[28] The person then attempts to avoid this object or to flee from it. The repression is a failure because it does not succeed in avoiding unpleasure; it merely changes the

---

[28] "Repression," *SE*, xiv, 155. The example Freud uses here is the "Case of Little Hans." See *Analysis of a Five-Year-Old-Boy, SE*, x, 3–149.

context in which this feeling will occur. In conversion hysteria the repression is partially successful in that the affect seems to disappear, or to be channeled into some physical or mental "innervation." The shaking of a hysteric's hand is an example of such a conversion of the psychical energy into a physical symptom. The indifference of this hysteria is in marked contrast to the profound anxiety of the phobic variety. That is, the person who is suffering from conversion hysteria may remain calm although a portion of his body is shaking. In obsessional neurosis repression seems at first to be successful, but usually begins to fail as an aggressive idea returns in the form of self-reproaches and ceremonial actions aimed at inhibition. Often in obsessional neurosis unpleasurable ideas will enter consciousness unaccompanied by the affect that they seem to "deserve." This affect is displaced on to some trivial activity or thought.

The presentation in "Repression" of the ways the repressed impulse is transformed and released is complemented, and qualified, by Freud's *Inhibitions, Symptoms and Anxiety*. In the earlier essay the dynamic perspective is centered on ambivalence. The outcome of a delicate balancing of forces and the "distance" of an idea from the original representative are key facets of the depth of ambivalence. These dimensions of the theory are not changed in the 1926 text, but some important additions are made. The first is that the motive force of repression is said to be the "fear of impending castration," and this fear becomes the prototypical experience for separation or object loss.[29] In little girls "castration" is central in terms of object loss and future relations to objects, but obviously not in terms of the fear of losing the penis. The importance of castration in the dynamic view of *Inhibitions, Symptoms and Anxiety* leads into a redefinition of the role of anxiety vis-à-vis repression. In earlier texts, Freud saw anxiety as the result of repression, the affect of the representative being displaced onto other ideas. In the later work he sees anxiety preceding the onset of repression as a dan-

[29] *Inhibitions, Symptoms and Anxiety, SE,* xx, 122, 129–131.

ger signal; as a sign, so to speak, that the instinctual demand is dangerous, that is, will lead to unpleasure. In other words, the ego reacts to the internal force as it would to an external one, and this reaction of an anxiety signal (which Freud speculates might be triggered by some mnemonic image, probably of castration) initiates a "flight" by the ego from the impulse. The flight consists in the ego's displacing the representative's energy (which will become further anxiety) so as to deny the idea admission to consciousness.

The economic view in "Repression" is fairly straightforward: primal repression stems from the ego (or preconscious, which can be regarded as a branch of the ego) as a prophylactic measure, and it is maintained, in part, by a displacement of energy from the impulse itself. The fact that repression demands a constant cathexis of energy is central in the early work, and the diminution of this expenditure during sleep is used in conjunction with the dream theory. In *Inhibitions, Symptoms and Anxiety*, Freud employs this same economic approach, but puts more of an emphasis on a dual role for the ego. The ego's economic strengths are shown in the later work, and Freud cautions against the view that our rational powers are slight in relation to the "daemonic forces within us." He comments:

> We were justified, I think, in dividing the ego from the id, for there are certain considerations which necessitate this step. On the other hand the ego is identical with the id, and is merely a specially differentiated part of it. If we think of this part by itself in contradistinction to the whole, or if a real split has occurred between the two, the weakness of the ego becomes apparent. But if the ego remains bound up with the id and indistinguishable from it, then it displays its strength.[30]

The emphasis on the economic strength of the ego's ties with the id leads into the new topographical perspective commonly known as the "second topography." In 1921 *The Ego and the Id* was published, using the terms Ucs., Pcs., and

[30] Ibid., 95.

Cs. less frequently than it used ego, superego, and id. The divisions are not parallel; the ego has unconscious and pre-conscious components to it, while the superego (the result of identification with the father, perhaps best thought of as a relatively severe conscience), although partly conscious is, for the most part, unconscious. The major difference between the topographical approaches used in "Repression" and in *Inhibitions, Symptoms and Anxiety* seems to be that consciousness has much closer ties to unconsciousness (and its energy) in the later work. Freud does not emphasize in the later work the sharp break between the parts of the mind that in 1915 was seen as a prerequisite for repression. To be sure, when repression occurs the break between the conscious and the unconscious is still spoken of. However, the later topography is more flexible than the earlier one as the concept of repression is integrated into the overall workings of the mind. Ego, superego, and id allow for the fluidity of consciousness with less confusion than did Ucs., Pcs., and Cs., because the latter terms could not take "conscious" as a predicate without oxymorons being created.

The entire theory of repression is concerned with a release of energy through a process of transformation. The instinctual representative that is denied access to consciousness does not disappear. Rather, it seeks avenues of release, of satisfaction. It is important to remember that the entity being repressed is a desire of the subject and not something foreign to him. As a result of repression, the desire is isolated, externalized, and finally transformed into a symptom. The symptom is often viewed by the subject as a "foreign body," but it remains a sign of the person's original desire. Hans's fear of horses, for example, was a displacement of his fear of castration and the aggressions he felt toward his father. The phobia remained, however, a sign of his original oedipal desires, which had been redirected from their original aim and object. The redirection of the desire allowed Hans to get some degree of satisfaction and avoid a portion of his anxiety. He displaced his aggression from his father to symbols of him and therefore minimized the fear of reprisal, and he could avoid horses (the symbol) with comparative ease. Both of these factors are the *secondary gains* achieved as a result of the transformation of the repressed impulse into other contexts.

The concept of secondary gains through symptom formation shows quite clearly how repression imposes severe limitations on the person's actions. The satisfaction derived from symptoms is no real compensation for the suffering occasioned by the way in which the symptom forces one to live. The symptom limits the functioning of the ego because it lies beyond the ego—beyond knowing. In *this* sense the symptom can certainly be considered a "foreign body." The lifting of the repression is the extending of understanding to include the process of transformation: an invitation to begin to act in the world. Freud comments on the ego that is paralyzed by the repeated attempts to turn away from the desire of the subject:

> The result of this process [secondary gain], which approximates more and more to a complete failure of the original purpose of defence, is an extremely restricted ego which is reduced to seeking satisfaction in the symptoms. The displacement of the distribution of forces in favor of satisfaction may have the dreaded final outcome of paralysing the will of the ego, which in every decision it has to make is almost as strongly impelled from one side as from the other.[31]

Freud would surely regard the ego that can seek satisfaction only in the symptoms, that is paralyzed by conflict, as pathological. The question that now arises is how this extreme pathological result of repression relates to "normal thought." It is clear that Freud regarded the dream as a pathological event,[32] and since the process of repression plays such a deep role in the transformation of the dream thoughts into their manifest content, one must conclude that the mechanism appears quite frequently in "normal" persons. In an important sense, to speak of a psyche without repression

[31] Ibid., 118.
[32] *The Interpretation of Dreams, SE,* IV, 101–102.

would be to speak of a psyche without an unconscious. Without repression, thoughts would always be available to consciousness; therefore they would fall into the category of preconscious. It is clear, then, from either topography, that Freud regarded repression as a universal, and probably a necessary, dimension of human mental activity. It must be noted, however, that he never, as far as I can tell, ventured to predict what particular manifestation will arise out of a repressed idea, but always attempted to discover the repressed idea from its particular manifestation. One sees here the same juxtaposition of history and interpretation that was found in the theory of dreams. Never becoming predictive, this approach is limited to making meaning out of our experience of the past, out of those events that have penetrated consciousness—limited to the mental.

Freud's work remains, if it is to retain the power of its insight, a system of interpretation and a theory of history. This means that it can search for the meanings of a particular sign (symptom, dream, action) by finding the dynamic elements of that sign's past which have generated its appearance. The questions that arise out of that meaning are extra-psycho-analytic. If psycho-analysis were to attempt to answer these questions, it would leave historical interpretation behind in favor of prophecy. And although he recognized the desire for prophets, Freud refused to satisfy it: "I have not the courage to rise up before my fellowmen as a prophet, and I bow to their reproach that I can offer them no consolation; for at bottom that is what they are demanding—the wildest revolutionaries no less passionately than the most virtuous believers."[33]

[33] *Civilization and Its Discontents, SE,* xxi, 145.

3

Infantile Sexuality

Where do all patients get the frightful perverse details
which are often as remote from their experience as
from their knowledge?

Freud to Fliess, October 3 and 4, 1897

Laymen and specialists alike have seen Freud's
theory of infantile sexuality as the most distinctive aspect of
his work. It is the part of psycho-analysis that is most difficult to accept, as well as the part to which Freud gives the
most detailed elaboration. The theory of infantile sexuality
completes his work as a theory of history, since it provides a
guide for the viewing of a person's past, a grid through which
we can understand the ways certain activities in this past
have an extraordinary effect on his later development.

This chapter is concerned with three topics: (a) the historical development of the theory of infantile sexuality in Freud's
thought up until the writing of *Three Essays on the Theory
of Sexuality*, (b) the theory of infantile sexual development,
(c) the role of sexuality as the material base of psycho-analysis and as the limit of psycho-analysis to the mental, to the
ideational components of desire, in contradistinction to its
physical components. The examination of these three topics
will demonstrate the role of historical interpretation in Freud's
work and will establish the foundation for the discussion, in
Section II, of the possibilities for human freedom through
sublimation or the transference.

No exhaustive attempt will be made here to trace the development of the idea of infantile sexuality through Freud's work. In the first section of this chapter I want to show only that infantile sexuality was not a presupposition with which he began, but rather was a discovery made through interpretation. Freud's difficulty in coming to the conclusions that sexuality plays an important role in the early years of childhood, and that it is part of the child's internal psychical development, has important implications for an understanding of the rest of the theory.

One of the first discussions in Freud's writings of the role of sexuality in the neuroses is in a paper of 1888, "Hysteria." In it Freud underscores the importance of "conditions related functionally to sexual life," specifically traumatic situations that center on fantasied or actual sexual encounters.[1] In a letter written to Wilhelm Fliess in December 1896, Freud underscored the importance of trauma as a form of seduction, stating: "It seems to me more and more that the essential point of hysteria is that it results from *perversion* on the part of the seducer, and *more and more* that heredity is seduction by the father."[2]

The "seduction theory" is based on assumptions that are in direct contradiction to Freud's later theory of infantile sexuality. The seduction theory held that a neurotic had passively undergone a sexual experience with an adult (the hysteric was said to have had this experience between the ages of three and four) and that this experience becomes "reactivated" with the onset of puberty. The sexual nature of the seduction is not at the time apprehended by the child; it has an effect only when that child becomes a sexual being after puberty. The memory of the scene is not repressed until after the sexual drive appears in puberty. The memory is then charged with libido and confined to the unconscious. It is crucial to see that Freud here views the child as a relatively asexual being. It is also important to note that the theory of seduction was based on reports of patients and that Freud

---

[1] *SE,* I, 51.
[2] "Extracts from the Fliess Papers," *SE,* I, 238–239.

believed in the reality of the seduction—and often took great pains to confirm the reports—rather than subjecting the reports themselves to interpretation.[3]

But in a letter dated September 21, 1897, Freud told Fliess that he had given up on the seduction theory. "I will confide in you at once the great secret that has been slowly dawning on me in the last few months," he wrote. "I no longer believe in my *neurotica*."[4] He then listed four reasons for this drastic theoretical revision. The first was his own lack of satisfaction with the therapeutic results he was getting, working with his theory of the etiology of the neuroses. He was having difficulty concluding his treatments and was uncertain about what caused such improvements as the patients experienced. The second reason was that the seduction theory implied an almost universal perversity among fathers, and such a belief seemed untenable, given all the available evidence.[5] The third reason Freud gives for discarding his theory of the neuroses is perhaps the most important for the later development of psycho-analysis: "Then, thirdly, the certain discovery that there are no indications of reality in the unconscious, so that one cannot distinguish between the truth and fiction that is cathected with the affect. (Thus, the possibility remained open that sexual phantasy invariably seizes upon the theme of parents.)"[6] One can see in the theory of the neuroses based

---

[3] See the comments on the role of seduction in Freud's theory as a whole in J. Laplanche and J.-B. Pontalis, *The Language of Psycho-Analysis*, trans. Donald Nicholson-Smith (New York, 1973), 393, 404–407.

[4] "Extracts from the Fliess Papers," *SE*, I, 259.

[5] Freud does not use the word "universal" in this regard, but he does point out that "the perversity would have to be immeasurably more frequent than the hysteria," and that hysteria itself was more widespread than expected. It is also clear that the difference between the hysteric and the normal person is one only of degree. See ibid., 260.

[6] Ibid. The last reason Freud gave for dropping the theory was its failure to shed any light upon the mechanisms at work in psychosis, where the childhood memory is never made conscious. The reference to psychosis can be seen as an early instance of applied psycho-analysis since Freud was not working with patients with this form of pathology. For a detailed account of Freud's complex motivations for abandoning the seduction the-

on seduction an attempt to trespass beyond what I have been calling the limit of psycho-analysis to the mental. That is, in trying to establish the reality of the seduction scene Freud was attempting to verify the mental by acquiring evidence from outside of it—trying to ascertain whether the seduction ever actually took place, rather than scrutinizing the meaning of the *report* of the seduction.[7] In later years his efforts would be concentrated on trying to understand the mental itself (through the signs that it presented) as deeply as possible. Meaning became independent of "indications of reality." In other words, with the abandonment of the seduction theory, Freud leaves behind a Rankean notion of history as a reconstruction of the past *as it really was*, and moves toward the mature psycho-analytic theory of history as making meaning out of memory in the service of the present.[8] Thus when Freud left the seduction theory behind, he was not in any sense giving up the connection of psycho-analysis to a theory of history. On the contrary, he in fact made it possible to situate the discipline in the tradition of thinking about history as meaningful memory that stretches from Vico, through Hegel and to Foucault.[9]

Although announcing his disbelief in the seduction theory in this letter to Fliess, Freud did not publicly drop it until 1905, in his *Three Essays on the Theory of Sexuality*. It is this work that systematically explores the role of sexuality in the development of the child, and the book remains, as James

---

ory, see William McGrath, *Freud's Discovery of Psychoanalysis: The Politics of Hysteria* (Ithaca, 1986), chaps. 4–6.

[7] See Ernest Jones, *The Life and Work of Sigmund Freud*, vol. 1 (New York, 1953), 262–277.

[8] "The mature psycho-analytic theory of history," however, still has its roots in the seduction theory. That is, Freud will at times still seek out "indications of reality" in order to inform the meanings generated within an analysis. This is particularly evident in his published case studies.

[9] Of course, Freud has great differences from these thinkers, as they also have differences from one another. None of them, however, has need of the equivalent of a "theory of seduction" to make sense out of change over time.

Strachey put it, "beside his *Interpretation of Dreams* as his most momentous and original contributions to human knowledge."[10] The information found in *Three Essays* is the result of at least fifteen years of theoretical and therapeutic work, and a substantial revision of ideas that went on between 1897 and 1905. The point here is simply that the theory of sexuality presented in *Three Essays* is not made up of "assumptions" that Freud created for psycho-analysis. *The Interpretation of Dreams*, written, for the most part, after the letter of 1897, does not explore the question of seduction at any length. However, the allusions to the Oedipus complex certainly foreshadow the change in theory which was to be announced in 1905.[11] *Three Essays on the Theory of Sexuality* reveals the findings of these early years of intellectual development, findings that Freud was to go back to and revise as psycho-analysis developed, but that remained fundamental to its coherence as a theory.

The order in which Freud places the three essays deserves some attention. The subject of infantile sexuality is dealt with only in the second essay; the first piece is entitled "The Sexual Aberrations," and the third, "The Transformations of Puberty." The aberrations are treated first, I think, because this order reflects the way the sexual nature of infantile development is discovered in the course of analysis. That is, the infantile period can be known only through the analysis of reports given in the present, not directly. It is certainly true that Freud later talked about the confirmation of the theoretical developments in *Three Essays* by means of the direct observation of children, but the substance of the book was determined by his interpretation of the reports of patients. The theory of infantile development is an attempt to make sense of these reports. The placement of "The Transformation of Puberty" in the third position reflects Freud's view of the importance of this period of development. Puberty is seen

---

[10] Strachey, "Editor's Note," in *Three Essays on Sexuality, SE,* vii, 126. References to page numbers of this work will in this chapter appear in my text.

[11] *The Interpretation of Dreams, SE,* iv, 261–267.

as the time when the sexual development of the infantile period becomes manifest in a displaced form alongside what is
usually regarded as the "normal" sexual drive. By placing the
study of puberty after that of infancy Freud allows the reader
clearly to see the way the patterns set at the earlier time
really continue to exist in some form in the manifest sexual
nature of the later period. Puberty marks the final organization of autoerotic infantile sexuality into a "social sexuality."
"With the arrival of puberty," Freud notes, "changes set in
which are destined to give infantile sexuality its final normal
shape. The sexual instinct has hitherto been predominantly
auto-erotic; it now finds a sexual object" (207).

"Infantile Sexuality," the second of the three essays, is the
most 'systematic account of Freud's views on the development of the infant's sexual drives. The pages that follow explicate this essay along with some additional material from
the later theory dealing with the Oedipus and castration
complexes. The material on these complexes is a necessary
supplement since Freud does not deal with these crucial
subjects in "Infantile Sexuality."

Freud begins his discussion of infantile sexuality with a
reference to the lack of any literature on the subject. Early in
the section he comments on the nature of what he calls "infantile amnesia": "There can, therefore, be no question of any
real abolition of the impressions of childhood, but rather of
an amnesia similar to that which neurotics exhibit for later
events, and of which the essence consists in a simple with-
holding of these impressions from consciousness, viz., in their
repression" (175).

Freud intimates that the significance of the early years of
childhood may indeed be great, given what is known about
repression. That is, if the amnesia is in fact a repression, then
that which is repressed—the early years—must be quite important. He goes so far as to speculate that it may indeed be
that "without infantile amnesia there would be no hysterical
amnesia" (177).

The amnesia surrounding infancy can be overcome by uncovering what had been unconscious memories of neurotics,

as well as by studying the frequently published reports about abnormal sexual activity (177). Usually, Freud tells the reader, one can see sexual activity in children around the third or fourth year, but it is before this time that decisive events occur in the person's sexual life. This is clear from the break that occurs in sexual activity around age five.[12] Freud remarks of this break: "It is during this period of total or only partial latency that are built up the mental forces which are later to impede the course of the sexual instinct and, like dams, restrict its flow—disgust, feelings of shame and the claims of aesthetic and moral ideals" (178). The break in sexual life that occurs at this time is, for Freud, also the origin of the amnesia about early infantile sexual life. The amnesia directs the psycho-analyst to go further back in time to the first years of life to see what is being dammed up and restricted.

The development of mental forces to impede sexuality cannot be attributed to the morality of civilization—or some component of it such as education—but must be understood as an organic development. This point is essential for Freud and is one of the reasons he denied that his work was in any way culture-specific. It should be noted that Freud regarded the process of sexual development as a fundamental component in the origin of civilization itself, and not merely as one of the results of civilization's historical development. Although he does not spend much time on the relation between sexuality and civilization in *Three Essays*, he does make reference to the later importance of this initial blockage of the sexual instinct:

> Historians of civilization appear to be at one in assuming that powerful components are acquired for every kind of cultural achievement by this diversion of sexual instinctual forces from sexual aims and their direction to new ones—a process that

[12] Freud does not give an age at this point, but it seems that five years would be approximately what he had in mind in light of the idea of the Oedipus complex (which will be discussed later in this chapter). The "break" in sexual activity is often referred to as the "latency stage."

deserves the name "sublimation." To this we would add, accordingly, that the same process plays a part in the development of the individual and we would place its beginning in the period of sexual latency of childhood. [178]

The first manifestation of infantile sexuality to which Freud turns is "thumb-sucking," which is the term Strachey uses to render the German *lutschen* (179).[13] Freud chooses this particular manifestation because it is so common, and because it is usually not regarded as having anything to do with the sexual. The activity is autoerotic; that is, the object of the action is (at least part of) the originator of the action. This auto-erotism is, Freud says, the "most striking feature of the sexual activity" (181).

Thumb-sucking is an example of an activity that combines the instincts for self-preservation (in this case, hunger) and the sexual instincts (in this case, autoerotic ones). Thumb-sucking is derived, of course, from the sucking involved in the ingestion of food, and it is an attempt to repeat the experience of satisfaction found in feeding time. Here one sees the first example of Freud's famous dictum: "The finding of an object is in fact a refinding of it" (222).[14] Thumb-sucking is an attempt to repeat a pleasurable activity; when the sucking brings satisfaction through the stimulation of the lips and the memory of earlier experiences, and is no longer connected with the taking in of nourishment, it is seen by Freud as a fully sexual event. Until that time it is an *anaclitic* activity—derived from and belonging to both the self-preservation and the sexual instincts. Jean Laplanche develops the concept of anaclisis and the "refinding problem" from Freud's work in his brilliant book *Life and Death in Psychoanalysis:*

We could elucidate this [the refinding problem] as follows: the object to be rediscovered is not the lost object, but its substi-

---

[13] See also the editor's footnote on p. 179.
[14] Here Freud also states, "There are thus good reasons why a child sucking at his mother's breast has become the prototype of every relation of love."

79

tute by displacement; the lost object is the object of self-preservation, of hunger, and the object one seeks to refind in sexuality is an object displaced in relation to that first object. [Milk
would be the first object, the breast would be the second, the
sexual, object.] From this, of course, arises the impossibility of
ever rediscovering the object, since the object which has been
lost *is not the same* as that which is to be rediscovered. Therein
lies the key to the essential "duplicity" situated at the very beginning of the sexual quest.[15]

Freud calls the sucking sexual because the person achieves
satisfaction from the tactile stimulation of the labial region
in a particular rhythm and from the memory (fantasy) of previous satisfactions. Labial gratification appeared to him to be
a prototype of later genital sexual satisfaction. "No one" he
wrote, "who has seen a baby sinking back satiated from the
breast and falling asleep with flushed cheeks and a blissful
smile can escape the reflection that this picture persists as a
prototype of the expression of sexual satisfaction in later life"
(182). As the lips come to be the vehicle for this type of pleasure again and again, they become an "erotogenic zone." Freud
defines this term as follows: "It is part of the skin or mucous
membrane in which stimuli of a certain sort evoke a feeling
of pleasure possessing a particular quality. . . . Thus the
quality of the stimulus has more to do with producing the
pleasurable feeling than has the nature of the part of the
body concerned" (183). Thus, the child comes to suck his
thumb in a sensual way solely for the pleasure he gets from
the stimulation of his labial region in a certain rhythm. In
later life, of course, the person will continue to derive pleasure from the stimulation of this zone through a variety of
techniques.

Thumb-sucking is the prototypical activity for what is
commonly referred to as the "oral stage." This phase is characterized by the child's relating to objects exclusively through
the mouth, parts of the body which can be said to function

[15]Laplanche, *Life and Death in Psychoanalysis*, trans. Jeffrey Mehlman
(Baltimore, 1976), 20.

like the mouth,[16] and eating. It must be noted that no detailed theory of stages appears in *Three Essays*, and that Freud never really gave a detailed account of what are now referred to as "libidinal stages," or "psychosexual stages." The idea does seem to be important to him, however, and it plays a major role in such a significant application of psycho-analysis as *Totem and Taboo*. A "stage," in Freud's work, refers to: (a) the primacy of a certain erotogenic zone where gratification occurs; (b) the organization of activity so that all the person's relations with objects are characterized by a particular association with the erotogenic zone.

To read Freud as having taken a linear view of the person's development is a mistake—a mistake common among commentators (especially psychologists).[17] This simplistic reading of Freud's theory of development views the stages as steps in the climb to maturity; steps that are either conquered or simply left behind. It is much more fruitful, and much more in line with what Freud said in his texts, to see the person's

[16]The expression "devouring someone with your eyes" is an example of how a function of the mouth can be displaced onto another part of the body.

[17]Liliane Frey-Rohn, a student of Jung's, takes the stance that Freud's work points to the active existence of the pregenital stages only in neurotics. Normal persons, she says, leave the early stages behind in the climb to adulthood. See Liliane Frey-Rohn, *From Freud to Jung: A Comparative Study of the Psychology of the Unconscious*, trans. F. Engreen and E. Engreen (New York, 1974), 146. Gordon Allport's almost total misreading of Freud includes his views on Freud's theory of development: *Becoming: Basic Considerations for a Psychology of Personality* (New Haven, 1955), 31–33. Abraham Maslow believed that his "psychology of health," wherein the person is promoted from stage to stage as a schoolchild is from grade to grade, was a complement of Freud's "psychology of pathology." For Maslow, only the unhealthy have a problem leaving a stage behind: *Toward a Psychology of Being*, 2d edition (New York, 1968), 23–24, 48–49. The psychoanalyst Benjamin Wolman offers another narrow and distorted perspective on Freud's theory of development in *The Unconscious Mind: The Meaning of Freudian Psychology* (Englewood Cliffs, N.J., 1968), 33–34, and chap. 7, especially 81. All these writers would like to deny the close connection between the normal and the abnormal that Freud maintained, and this affects their readings of Freud's theory of development. In this regard see Russell Jacoby, *Social Amnesia: A Critique of Conformist Psychology from Adler to Lang* (Boston, 1975), passim, and Gerald Izenberg, *The Existentialist Critique of Freud: The Crisis of Autonomy* (Princeton, 1976), chaps. 5 and 6.

development in dialectical terms.[18] That is to say, the stages continue to exist after they have been passed through, and succeeding stages are built upon preceding ones without destroying them. Furthermore, it is clear that Freud saw that the stages continued to exert some influence through their existence in the unconscious (in character traits, for example); otherwise, there would be no way to know of their existence through interpretation. The stages remain integrated, and early phases are not left behind when maturity is reached.[19] A naive linear view often implies sharp breaks with one's history (especially when the genital stage is reached), and this is surely not what Freud had in mind. I showed above in the discussion of repression that the unconscious impulses do not decay and fade away but remain quite active while not in consciousness. Something similar to this must be true of the unconscious existence of the pregenital stages.[20] The naive linear reading of Freud avoids the unconscious existence of the infantile, one of the most central of Freud's findings. This avoidance is in direct contradiction to the theory of repression discussed above because it denies that the repressed (infantile) impulse continues to strive for satisfaction in an active way.

To characterize the oral stage one can simply examine thumb-sucking. The activity is at first attached to a "vital somatic function," autoerotic, centered on satisfaction derived from the labial area (182). In all the stages the aim of the sexual drive will be to release tension centered in a particu-

---

[18]The whole of *Three Essays* supports a dialectical reading of the theory of development, especially Freud's remarks on the diphasic choice of an object (200). See also Freud, *Introductory Lectures on Psycho-Analysis*, SE, xvi, lectures xx and xxi, especially 309–310, 317–321; Freud, *An Outline of Psycho-Analysis*, SE, xxiii, chap. 3, especially 155–156; Freud, *Group Psychology and the Analysis of the Ego*, SE, xviii, 111, 138; Freud, *Civilization and Its Discontents*, SE, xxi, 68–73; and Freud, *Totem and Taboo*, SE, xiii, 88–90.

[19]This should be especially clear from Freud's discussion of "infantile amnesia" (175–177).

[20]Freud explicitly refers to the repression of the infantile impulses in many places, for example, in *An Outline of Psycho-Analysis*, SE, xxiii, 155. See also Freud, "The Dissolution of the Oedipus Complex," SE, xix, 177.

lar area of the body by means of a controlled stimulation of that area (184).

Freud turns his attention in the next section of the essay to "Masturbatory Sexual Practices" and, first, to the infant's erotic concentration on the anal zone. It is at this time (usually around age two) that the child learns to have greater control over his bowel movements and to take pleasure in that control. The pressure of the feces on the mucous membrane and the muscular contractions that occur with defecation present the infant with an array of intense and stimulating sensations in the anal area which he can learn to master and control. Since the child is learning to produce pleasure when he so desires by mastering what had been automatic movements, Freud refers to the erotic concentration on the anal zone as masturbatory.

The anal stage of development has drawn much attention from psychoanalysts in Freud's time and more recently. In later work, Freud attributed three main character traits to those who were particularly influenced by the anal stage: orderliness, parsimoniousness, and obstinacy.[21] The process of defecation is crucial for the way the infant will later deal with separation from objects and with the voluntary giving of objects to other people. The feces are the child's first gift to the world and also involve the separation of a part of the person from the larger whole (186). The anal stage becomes increasingly important as castration—the ultimate separation for Freud—begins to play a role in development. The experience of separation in the anal period becomes relevant again— one might say "reactivated"—in the later phase. The importance of anality for later development will not be discussed at any length here, but how this phase influences the subsequent history of the person shows further why the stages have the integrative relationship stressed above.

After the discussion of the role of the anus as an eroto-

---

[21] See Freud's 1908 essay, "Character and Anal Erotism," *SE*, ix, 167–177. In *Civilization and Its Discontents* (1930), Freud lists the anal traits as "parsimony, a sense of order and cleanliness," *SE*, xxi, 96–97.

genic zone, Freud distinguishes between two types of infantile masturbation involving the genitals. The first is undergone by the child in a more or less passive way. That is, the
little boy or girl has his or her genitals stimulated by the
touch of a guardian during any number of cleaning or dress-
ing routines. This stimulation leads the child to desire a repetition of these activities for the sake of the sexual pleasure
that comes along with them. In a short time the child begins
actively to manipulate his or her genitals to create these
pleasurable sensations (this, usually around age four). At this
point external contingencies may have an important effect
on development, seduction being one of the more important
of these contingencies.

Freud characterizes the child at this time as having the
capacity for "polymorphous perversity," which indicates that
the child has the ability to derive sexual satisfaction from
various types of stimulation to almost any area of his body.
Often a sibling, guardian, or playmate will initiate the child
into some sexual activity that would be considered deviant
by society. Indeed, Freud claims that there exists a "disposition to perversions of every kind" and that this disposition is
"a general and fundamental human characteristic" (191).[22]
There are several component instincts to sexuality that play
an important role in childhood. The drives of scopophilia
(pleasure from seeing sexual activity) exhibitionism, and cruelty (both passive and active) are examples of complements
to sexuality that may become quite intense around the ages
of four and five.

It must be remembered that, for the most part, the sexual
instincts continue to seek their gratification through autoerotic means during this time. Objects may be presented by
others (Freud calls these others "seducers"), but the child
attempts to continue to satisfy what has become a large va-

---

[22] Freud viewed perversion as a preoccupation with a way of seeking sexual satisfaction that was not combined with heterosexual coitus. It is fairly
obvious from what is quoted here, and indeed from the whole of "Infantile
Sexuality," that "normal" sexuality rests, in a fundamental sense, upon the
repression of "perverse" desire.

riety of desires without the aid of another person. For example, the child will intently *watch himself* manipulate his or her own genitals so as to satisfy both the desire to exhibit his or her private parts and the wish to observe a person engaged in sexual activity.

Freud introduced the term "phallic phase" in a paper written in 1923 to describe a time in which the polymorphous nature of the sexual life of both boys and girls begins to be organized around the phallus. The section of "Infantile Sexuality" that discusses the sexual researches of children (a section added to the main body of the text in 1915) deals with some of the major events that Freud was to place under the phallic phase in his later work. It is evident from this section that Freud in 1915 conceived of the phallus as being the primary element in the life of the child from ages five to seven. As far as the little boy is concerned, Freud says: "It is self-evident to a male child that a genital like his own is to be attributed to everyone he knows, and he cannot make its absence tally with his picture of these other people." And of little girls: "They are ready to recognize them [the male genitals] immediately and are overcome by envy for the penis— an envy culminating in the wish, which is so important in its consequences, to be boys themselves" (195).

As if the theory of early infantile sexuality does not create enough of an indignant reaction to psycho-analysis, Freud's theory of development in the phallic stage raises a host of new problems. First, there is the Oedipus complex—certainly *the* crucial theoretical component in Freud's work— and the theoretical difficulties that the triangular structure of the child's desire entails. Second, there is the role of castration, the presence and absence of the penis, which raises important theoretical and explicitly political questions. Both these topics are focal points for Freud as well; that is, they are points at which central problems for the theory as a whole arise, points that seem to be of ultimate importance for the therapeutic application of psycho-analysis as well as its coherence as a discipline.

One cannot really overestimate the importance of the Oe-

dipus complex in Freud's conception of human development. He called the complex "the nucleus of the neuroses"
(226n),[23] and believed that it was the most important element
in the transition from the predominantly autoerotic infantile
period to the object choices that would come to characterize
the person's mature years. As he emphatically says in a 1920
footnote in *Three Essays*, the Oedipus complex "represents
the peak of infantile sexuality, which, through its after-ef-
fects, exercises a decisive influence on the sexuality of adults.
Every new arrival on this planet is faced by the task of mastering the Oedipus complex; anyone who fails to do so falls
a victim to neurosis" (226n). There is, however, no systematic
detailed account of the Oedipus complex in Freud's corpus,
and in *Three Essays* he does not even place the occurrence
of the complex in the infantile period![24] If one can say (I
believe one can, and helpfully so) that Freud's writings contain a final version of the Oedipus complex in the little boy,
it would be something like the following: At age five, when
the child's sexual activity begins to be organized around the
phallus, the little boy takes his mother (as he perceives her,
of course) as a love object. That is, he wants to make use of
his mother to satisfy his erotic desires, and he wants to have
the mother available for this purpose at all times when the
desires are present. Since the father is the child's rival in this
regard, the little boy desires the death of his father so that
he can have exclusive access to his mother. This is the POSI-
TIVE side of the oedipal situation. The NEGATIVE side is the
boy's identification with the mother—this, through his
preoedipal attachment to her as a source of pleasure—and a
desire for his perception of the father as a love object. The
boy's desire to have the father possess him leads the child

[23] And Freud, *Introductory Lectures on Psycho-Analysis*, *SE*, xvi, 337 and
note. In *Totem and Taboo*, Freud says that "the beginnings of religion, mor-
als, society and art converge in the Oedipus complex": *SE*, xiii, 156.

[24] No mention of the Oedipus complex appears in "Infantile Sexuality."
However, from the footnote just quoted and from the late essays on sexuality, it seems clear that Freud conceived of the Oedipus complex as being
the apex of the infantile period.

to have hostile feelings toward his mother.[25] It must be noted that the positive and negative aspects of the Oedipus complex are usually both present in a single child, and that the resolution of the complex—a coming to terms with the taboo against incest—usually favors one or the other poles (the little boy will usually identify with the father) but not to the complete exclusion of the other.

The Oedipus complex is resolved in little boys through the threat of castration, actual or fantasied. The child's hatred of the father (more accurately, his conception of the rivalry with the father) leads to the belief that the father will punish him or try to eliminate the boy as a rival. The punishment (and effective elimination) is conceived of as the taking away of the source of the boy's greatest pleasure—the means for obtaining pleasure through self- and motherly manipulation—his penis. The boy, out of fear, withdraws his object cathexes from his mother and enters into a period of sexual latency. As a way of dealing with perceived aggression from the father the little boy identifies with him; the boy becomes the powerful "large-penised father." Here one sees a typical psychic maneuver of moving from the passive position to the active position—through the identification the boy becomes the one who can be aggressive instead of being the person who fears aggression. Also, by being the father he may "safely" keep some attachment to the mother, although he will not have exclusive access to her. With identification, the world of the father becomes the world of the son. Through identification the son *creates himself* as heir to the father as ruler.

As the castration complex marks the beginning of the dissolution of the Oedipus complex for the boy, it initiates the triangular situation for the girl. The perception of being castrated tears the little girl away from her mother, who, because she too has no penis, has been devalued in the child's eyes. This leaves open the possibility that the father will be-

---

[25]The two sides of the Oedipus conflict are not really symmetrical. Identification with the mother can easily take place because of the child's intense attachment to her during the first two years of life; there is never the intense rivalry with the mother that the boy feels with the father.

come the girl's love object. Freud elaborated on the specific nature of the female Oedipus complex in the 1931 essay "Female Sexuality," and that elaboration is worth explicating briefly. What is most distinct about Freud's treatment of the girl is the emphasis he puts on the preoedipal period to explain the later situation. Like the boy, she takes her mother as her first love object and sees her father as a rival for mother's love.[26] This view of the father never contains the depth of aggressiveness perceived by a male child because a *threat* of castration by the father never enters the picture. The girl's attachment to her mother is severed only when she perceives herself as having been deprived of a penis like the boy's and of the mother as having been similarly deprived. Freud concludes: "The child invariably regards castration in the first instance as a misfortune peculiar to herself; only later does she realize that it extends to certain other children and lastly to certain grown-ups. When she comes to understand the general nature of the characteristic, it follows that femaleness—and with it, of course, her mother—suffers a great depreciation in her eyes."[27]

The little girl's sexual life is marked by severe disappointment. The loss of self-regard that comes with the consciousness of oneself as castrated is similar to the boy's experience of comparing the father's penis to his own. There is, however, a crucial difference in their reactions to this experience. The boy has recourse to identification with the father because the fact that each has a penis implies a certain relationship between them. The girl cannot identify with her mother in any significant sense because of her low opinion of this parent. More important, the little boy turns from his passive condition of being afraid of castration to the active position of being the father. The female child, on the other hand, *remains in the passive position*, her active drives almost totally frustrated by her realization of castration. The

[26] "Female Sexuality," *SE*, XXI, 226.
[27] Ibid., 233.

female Oedipus complex is essentially passive; the male, active. For this reason, *the passive experience is the feminine experience.* As Freud remarks in "Female Sexuality": "The transition to the father-object is accomplished with the help of the passive trends in so far as they have escaped the catastrophe [the realization of castration]. The path to the development of femininity now lies open to the girl."[28]

It is clear from this brief summary of the Oedipus and castration complexes that they are fundamental to organizing the autoerotic sexual drives into a more or less adult way of relating to objects. Although I do not want to discuss what some have called "Freud's sexism" or, for that matter, the "theory's sexism" at any length, a word must be said about this subject. I have refrained throughout this entire section from evaluating Freud's theory and have instead merely presented aspects of it along with pointing out some difficulties that the theory seems to engender. I shall not criticize Freud's ideas concerning infantile sexuality. However, the particular criticism that psycho-analysis has its origins in a "Victorian" and "bourgeois" culture and is therefore necessarily sexist demands a short response. This criticism is particularly shortsighted in that it denies the possibility of self-consciousness in history. As Russell Jacoby notes, this type of criticism is based on "an awareness of historical transformation which ideologically stops short of itself; its own viewpoint is considered neutral and absolute truth, outside—not inside—history."[29] To label Freud "a genius stuck in his own time" or a "prisoner of culture" is a simpleminded attempt to deny the meaning of history, while claiming to be historically meaningful.[30] One may, of course, find the theory im-

---

[28] Ibid., 239.

[29] Jacoby, *Social Amnesia*, 2.

[30] This criticism is an old one, and it takes many forms. For examples of the claim that Freud was "stuck in his own time" see: Karen Horney, *New Ways in Psychoanalysis* (New York, 1939), 37, and Clara Thompson, *Psychoanalysis: Evolution and Development* (New York, 1950), 132–135. For critical appraisals of the claim, see Juliet Mitchell, *Psychoanalysis and Feminism* (New York, 1974), 420, and Jacoby, *Social Amnesia*, 1–2.

plausible or find that it does not give meaning to history, but those are other matters.[31]

What I want to emphasize here is that Freud's theory of the development of the female is, like the rest of his work, a theory based on the interpretation of the analysand's history, not on the nature of being female. The "castration complex" and "penis envy" are ways in which the rule of patriarchy and the passivity (one might even say "pacification") of women can be understood. As the son creates himself as heir to the father, the daughter *is (re)created* as heir to the mother and may be dominated in the same way. It is important to remember that the girl perceives the place of degradation that the mother occupies as resulting from the father's power and therefore may later have the opportunity to refuse to fill that place. This perception quickly becomes unconscious in childhood, but it does not decay. Rather, as a repressed impulse, it "proliferates in the dark." It is legitimate to regard the theory of female development—which is based, like the rest of the theory, on interpretations of the histories of individual development within a patriarchal culture—as an excavation of that perception and hence providing the opportunity to set the precondition for the refusal to remain passive.[32]

[31]A review of the psychoanalytic revisions of Freud's view of female development is not appropriate here. Some important texts in this regard are Janine Chasseguet-Smirgel, "Freud and Female Sexuality: The Consideration of Some Blind Spots in the Exploration of the 'Dark Continent'," *IJP*, 57 (1976), 275–286, with discussions following; J. Chasseguet-Smirgel, ed., *Female Sexuality* (Ann Arbor, 1970); Jean Strouse, ed., *Women and Analysis: Dialogues on Psychoanalytic Views of Femininity* (New York, 1974); Roy Schaefer, "Problems in Freud's Psychology of Women," *JAPA*, 22 (1974), 459–485; Irene Fast, "Developments in Gender Identity: Gender Differentiation in Girls," *IJP*, 60 (1979), 443–453; Nancy Chodorow, *The Reproduction of Mothering: Psychoanalysis and the Sociology of Gender* (Berkeley, 1978); Dorothy Dinnerstein, *The Mermaid and the Minotaur: Sexual Arrangements and Human Malaise* (New York, 1976); and, on Lacan and feminism, Jane Gallop, *The Daughter's Seduction: Feminism and Psychoanalysis* (Ithaca, 1984). A very brief discussion of the feminist political critique of psychoanalysis is found at the end of Section III, below.

[32]Juliet Mitchell remarks in *Psychoanalysis and Feminism* (xiii): "However it may be used, psychoanalysis is not a recommendation *for* a patriarchal

Presentation of the Oedipus complex has logically inter-
vened in my explication of "Infantile Sexuality," two sections
of which, "The Phases of Development of the Sexual Organization" and "The Sources of Infantile Sexuality,"[33] remain to
be discussed. In the former the oral phase, which Freud calls
the "cannibalistic pregenital sexual organization" is succinctly presented: "Here sexuality has not yet been separated
from the ingestion of food; nor are opposite currents within
the activity differentiated. The *object* of both activities is the
same; the sexual *aim* consists in the incorporation of the object—the prototype of a process which, in the form of identification, is later to play such an important psychological
part" (198). The second stage of development, the sadistic-
anal organization, is marked by the beginnings of the opposition between active and passive sexual aims. The free emp-
tying of the bowels involves passive gratification through the
anus, and the active part of the sexual aim is seen in the
attempt intentionally to control the expulsion of the feces. In
the anal phase one sees the rather marked appearance of
ambivalence, the stage in which "an opposing pair of instincts are to develop to an approximately equal extent" (199).
"Ambivalence," a term first used by Paul Bleuler, is especially
important for psycho-analysis, as should be clear from the
discussion of the phallic and oedipal periods above.[34] In situations of ambivalence, the person begins to attempt some

---

order, but an analysis *of* one." Mitchell makes the point again and again
that Freud's work is descriptive, not prescriptive. Her discussion in *Psycho-
analysis and Feminism* is deeply influenced by the work of Lacan. In France,
psychoanalysis has had a more nuanced connection with feminism than
in the United States. For a critical appraisal of Mitchell's incomplete use of
Lacan, see Jane Gallop, "The Ghost of Lacan, the Trace of Language," *Dia-
critics*, 5 (Winter 1975), 18–24. See also Amy F. Galen "Rethinking Freud on
Female Sexuality: A Look at the New Orthodox Defense," *Psychoanalytic
Review*, 66 (1979), 173–186; and Elizabeth A. Waites, "Female Self Representation and the Unconscious: A Reply to Amy Galen," *Psychoanalytic Review*,
69 (1982), 29–41.

[33]The first was added to the main body of the text in 1915; the second
was in the original.

[34]Bleuler was in charge of psychiatry at the Burghoelzi hospital, Zurich,
and was Jung's teacher there.

kind of object choice and is not merely acting in accordance with autoerotic desire.

Freud ends this discussion of the phases of sexuality by commenting on the "diphasic" nature of the object choice. By "diphasic" he means that our infantile desire and postpubertal desire are divorced from each other by a period of sexual latency and psychical repression. Here one sees the dialectical nature of Freud's phases quite clearly; that is, one sees that the stages are negated and preserved. Freud comments on the later activity of "infantile sexual longings":

> The resultants of infantile object-choice are carried over into the later period. They either persist as such or are revived at the actual time of puberty. But as a consequence of the repression which has developed between the two phases they prove unutilizable. Their sexual aims have become mitigated and they now represent what may be described as the "affectionate current" of sexual life. Only psycho-analytic investigation can show that behind this affection, admiration and respect there lie concealed the old sexual longings of the infantile components which have now become unserviceable. [200]

Psycho-analytic investigation, by laying bare the nature of a "mature" object choice, makes the act of choosing more meaningful by helping the person grasp that the choosing situation itself can be integrated into a coherent history which shows the connections between choice in the present and a significant past.

The last section of "Infantile Sexuality" deals with the sources of the sexual drive itself. Freud identifies three areas from which the drive arises: "a) as a reproduction of a satisfaction experienced in connection with other organic processes, b) through appropriate peripheral stimulation of erotogenic zones and c) as an expression of certain 'instincts' (such as the scopophilic instinct and the instinct of cruelty) of which the origin is not yet completely intelligible" (200). He concludes the essay by stating the three general ways in which sexual experience occurs: (a) from the specific qualitative stimulation of sensory surfaces, (*b*) from the quantity of the excitation produced by certain internal processes, (*c*) from a displaced form of either *a* or *b*, such as mechanical excitations, muscular activity, affective processes, or intellectual work. Freud referred to these forms as "sublimations" of the sexual instinct (206).

The theory of infantile sexuality is crucial for psycho-analysis because it provides the material base of the discipline while remaining within the domain of the mental, of memory and its meanings. In the beginning of this chapter Freud's search for "indications of reality" was discussed. When Freud gave up this search—that is, when he gave up the seduction theory—he had recognized that the proper object for psychoanalytic study was the mental and that the discipline would take him to the depths of mind and its functions. The sexual drive is the border of the mental, where the somatic and the psychic begin to merge. It must be remembered that the mental is known only through the interpretation of the analysand's discourse—the embodiment of the mental. Interpretation leads from the signs given by the analysand to the dynamics that gave rise to those signs and finally to the relationship between these dynamics and their expression. This path of interpretation makes available the meaning of the past in its relationship to the present, the truth of history that ends in the present.

The material nature of the sexual drives stems from their original overlapping with the self-preservative drives—what I have previously called the physiological. In this original state all actions are automatic reactions; there is nothing else but material, what Ricoeur calls "Thingness." The objects that the infant begins to relate to (perceive) are not as yet sexual objects, but are experienced by anaclisis. Freud describes the anaclitic relation between the instincts: "The first auto-erotic sexual satisfactions are experienced in connection with vital functions which serve the purpose of self-preservation. The sexual instincts are at the outset attached to the satisfaction of the ego-instincts; only later do they become independent

93

of these."[35] The sexual nature of the object is based on a metonymic relationship with the original self-preservative sexual object.[36] The child getting satisfaction autoerotically through the fantasy of labial stimulation is getting sexual satisfaction, but the basis for that desire lies in the physiological need for nourishment. *The sexual desire is based upon the physiological need, upon the material, but is itself a mental phenomenon.* Desire becomes a basis for consciousness, for humanness. Psycho-analysis contributes to our understanding only in its efforts to grasp the development of the dynamic of consciousness and desire. It interpretes the manifestation of this dynamic in signs to rediscover the lost meaning of desire, the lost humanness of the subject.

As we have seen, the concepts of history and interpretation play large roles in the most important aspects of Freud's theory. In the dream theory the combination of these elements created what has been called a Freudian hermeneutics, a system of interpretation that examined the past to understand the meaning it had for the choices being made in the present, for the possibilities for freedom. For Freud, showing the connections between the wishes in the dream and one's past coincided with showing that the dream had a meaning. By grasping the meaning of the dream, the royal road to the unconscious, one was in a better position to choose with fuller knowledge of the ways choice emerged from the past and pointed toward the future. One moved closer to freedom.

The theory of repression is "interpretive" in its attempt to penetrate the past and to understand the aim of desire and the purposes served by the blockage of the consciousness of desire. All this "penetration," this "filling of gaps," was Freud's attempt to find the meaning of the past through interpretation, not to predict what gaps might arise in the future. His effort in the theory of repression was to provide a tool for

---

[35] "On Narcissism: An Introduction," *SE,* xiv, 87.
[36] See Laplanche, *Life and Death in Psychoanalysis,* 20, 88.

the lifting of the veil of ignorance from the face of the past, but his work gave no answers as to how one was to react to what was seen.

In the theory of infantile sexuality the role of psycho-analysis as a tool for understanding the past was clearly evident. The place of history and interpretation is clear even in the order of Freud's presentation in his only book on sexuality, *Three Essays on the Theory of Sexuality*. The importance of the sexual as both material and mental and Freud's dialectical view of development are crucial here because they show why psycho-analysis is concerned with the past. Since nothing really dies in the unconscious, the past continues to be preserved within the depths of the mental. Only by understanding the past, then, can one understand the temporal depth of the "here and now," since the former continues to have an *active* existence within the person. If one does not grasp the meaning of this "past," how, indeed, could freedom be possible?

The most general conclusion that can be drawn from the explication of the theory of dreams, the theory of repression, and the theory of infantile sexuality is that Freud's work is first and foremost a theory of history. As a theory of history, the work aims at establishing a more complete consciousness in the person than had previously existed; such a consciousness is a precondition of freedom. The following section will discuss how this theory of history becomes relevant to action in the present.

SECTION II

ACKNOWLEDGING
AND FREEDOM

4

Sublimation and the Transference

> The radical heteronomy that Freud's discovery shows
> gaping within man can never again be covered over
> without whatever is used to hide it being profoundly
> dishonest.
>
> Jacques Lacan, *Ecrits: A Selection*

> As it is not the brute, but only man that thinks, he
> only—and only because he is a thinking being—has
> Freedom.
>
> Hegel, *The Philosophy of History*

My explication of some of Freud's major texts on dream interpretation, repression, and infantile sexuality has shown how psycho-analysis uses historical interpretation as a vehicle for making sense out of the development of conflicts. This chapter will explore the way the theory of history is completed in a choosing situation in the present. This choosing situation I take to be the end of psycho-analysis, its limits as a coherent system of interpretation. The concepts of sublimation and the transference, both crucially related to choice, will be examined here in detail. The transference will be shown to be a more complete path toward the possibility of change than sublimation: complete in the sense of being both fundamental and final. As a relationship which manifests the repetitions, defenses, and frustrations that characterize the pathological facets of normal living, the transference phenomenon offers the possibility of the negation (*Aufhebung*) of these facets.

Freud's concepts of sublimation and the transference are closely connected with the presence of contradiction in the person's life—active contradiction, painful conflict. The degree of contradiction between the person's desires and the world that confronts them is the key to whether the opportunity for negation found in the transference is to be realized. In other words, radical activity is initiated as the result of struggle, and this only when the person sees that the sacrifice necessary to make the radical change is outweighed by the potential gratification of the change. Although his liberal apologists would like to find it there, there is no basis in Freud's work for the assumption that psycho-analysis can lead only to small changes in a person's situation—to adaptation—since this minimizes the sacrifice that action necessitates. The basis for this assumption is to be found in the belief that our lives do not confront us with contradictions that are deep enough to necessitate radical activity aimed at the creation of a world in which desire can be gratified without being profoundly manipulated.[1]

There is no general theory of sublimation in Freud's writings, although he uses the concept often and it seems to be one of the most central mental processes with which psycho-analysis is confronted. Sublimation is the release of infantile sexual impulses in nonsexual, socially acceptable forms.[2] As Laplanche and Pontalis note, there are two important senses of what Freud called *Sublimierung:* "Introduced into psycho-analysis by Freud, this term evokes the sense

[1] There will be some "slippage," to use Laplanche's term, in this chapter between the way sublimation and the transference relate to the individual and the way these concepts relate to the group. The overriding concern in this chapter is with the former.

[2] For careful accounts of how Freud used the concept of sublimation, see: Harry B. Levy, "A Critique of the Theory of Sublimation," *Psychiatry,* 2 (1939), 239–270; Peter Madison, *Freud's Concept of Repression and Defence, Its Theoretical and Observational Language* (Minneapolis, 1961), 77–82; and Jean Laplanche, *Problematiques III: La sublimation* (Paris, 1980).

'sublime' has when it is used, particularly in the fine arts, to qualify works that are grand or uplifting. It also evokes the sense 'sublimation' has for chemistry: the procedure whereby a body is caused to pass directly from a solid to a gaseous state."[3] These two senses of sublimation remained important throughout Freud's writings on the topic for over thirty years.

The first published use of the term "sublimation" occurs in *Three Essays on the Theory of Sexuality*. In a passage quoted above,[4] Freud briefly discussed the relationship of the sexual instincts to the development of civilization. Civilization diverts the energies of the sexual instincts to aims that are compatible with its development. The 1905 description of sublimation is connected with both Laplanche and Pontalis's senses of the concept. In other words, the sexual impulses are the solid that is changed into the rarified, sublime, form essential to the march of society.

Although Freud certainly viewed this release of sexual energy as "grand or uplifting," it is clear in *Three Essays* that he also recognized that the individual paid a price for this socially acceptable process of transformation:

> What is it that goes to the making of these constructions which are so important for the growth of a civilized and normal individual? They probably emerge at the cost of the infantile sexual impulses themselves. Thus the activity of those impulses does not cease even during this period of latency, though their sexual energy is diverted, wholly or in great part, from their sexual use and directed to other ends.[5]

To put this "cost" in more concrete terms: the process of sublimation denies the sexual satisfaction of the infantile sexual impulses, and the gratification attained when these impulses are satisfied in their new form is the result of a compromise—sexual impulses remain in some sense un-

---

[3] J. Laplanche and J. B. Pontalis, *The Language of Psycho-Analysis*, trans. Donald Nicholson-Smith (New York, 1973), 432.

[4] Above, p. 78–79.

[5] *Three Essays on the Theory of Sexuality*, SE, VII, 178.

gratified. These unsatisfied unconscious impulses remain in the unconscious; they are the residue, one may say, of the transformation from the solid to the gas, from the material to the sublime.

Freud's most important in-depth study of sublimation is in *Leonardo Da Vinci and a Memory of His Childhood* (1910). Here Freud gives his reader a portrait of a hero of civilization, a figure who can be seen as, in many ways, the highest product of the forces of society. The psycho-analytic study does not take issue with this common view of Leonardo. It does, however, reveal that these forces are suppressive and that they divert some of the individual's deepest desires. The activity that results from this "diversion" is activity that originates from frustrated desire, impulses that cannot pursue their primary aim. Freud compares the transformation of sublimation to physical changes, noting that "a conversion of psychical instinctual force into various forms of activity can perhaps no more be achieved without loss than a conversion of physical forces."[6] What is lost in the process of sublimation is not the impulses themselves, but their full satisfaction. The ungratified impulses remain in the unconscious.

Leonardo's infancy, Freud explains, was characterized by an extended period of intimacy with his mother, due to the absence of his father (Leonardo was an illegitimate child). Freud interprets a memory of the artist's as a passive homosexual fantasy. Leonardo desired to remain in the passive position of an infant with its mother, but this desire did not reach consciousness in direct form. "The boy represses his love for his mother," Freud writes; "he puts himself in her place, identifies himself with her, and takes his own person as a model in whose likeness he chooses the new objects of his love. In this way he has become a homosexual."[7] The other important facet of Leonardo's early years for Freud is the intense development of what in *Three Essays* was referred to as the instinct for knowledge or research. This drive,

---

[6] *Leonardo Da Vinci and a Memory of His Childhood*, SE, xi, 75.
[7] Ibid., 100.

which appears for the first time in the phallic stage, is already a sublimated form of the impulse for mastery and scopophilia.[8] The instinct for knowledge in Leonardo was reinforced because of the missing father, who complicated the riddle of where babies come from for the young child.

As Leonardo grew to maturity the complicated forces of his childhood were subjected to repression, sublimation, and other defenses, in the effort to compromise between the demands of civilization and desire[9] as well as among his own conflicting desires. His art work was one example of the results of these compromises, gratification is achieved through representation and looking, rather than through a direct satisfaction of homosexual or incestuous desires. Freud notes that artistic creation brings about a certain release of tension: "We must be content to emphasize the fact—which it is hardly any longer possible to doubt—that what an artist creates provides at the same time an outlet for his sexual desire; and in Leonardo's case . . . that heads of laughing women and beautiful boys—in other words, representations of his sexual objects—were notable among his first artistic endeavors."[10]

The instinct for knowledge also became sublimated in Leonardo's later life. That is to say, he was no longer investigating overtly sexual material, but he continued to have a deep interest in science and theoretical matters generally. Freud quotes a remark of Leonardo's in which it does not take much effort to see the sexual content of his search for knowledge: "For in truth great love springs from great knowledge of the beloved object, and if you know it but little you will be able to love it only a little or not at all." Interpreting

---

[8]The section of *Three Essays* that deals with the instinct for knowledge, "The Sexual Researches of Childhood," was added to the main body of the text in 1915, after *Leonardo* was written. Freud had already spoken of sexual satisfaction from intellectual work in the first edition of *Three Essays*, *SE*, vii, 204–206.

[9]Civilization is used in this chapter in a very broad sense, the sense in which Freud uses it: the sum of all those achievements and inhibitions that distinguish human beings from the other animals. See *Civilization and Its Discontents*, *SE*, xxi, 89.

[10]*Leonardo*, *SE*, xi, 132–133.

this statement as not about how people *do* love, but as Leonardo's view about how they *ought* to love, Freud continues: "Leonardo, then, could only have meant that the love practised by human beings was not of the proper and unobjectionable kind: one *should* love in such a way as to hold back the affect, subject it to the process of reflection and only let it take its course when it has stood up to the test of thought."[11]

The process of sublimation that Leonardo's instinct for knowledge goes through (and this, indeed, is a resublimation) reveals the dilemmas within the mechanism as a whole. A substitution occurs in sublimation: the aim of the instinct is redirected.[12] In other words, the original impulse, since it cannot be satisfied in its original form without painful consequences, finds outlets in more acceptable forms.[13] What is unusual about sublimation, in contradistinction to the other defenses, is that there is a considerable amount of release involved, so that the residue of the instinct that is left unsatisfied cannot create the frustrations that lead to pathology. This aspect of the process leads Freud consistently to distinguish between the concepts of sublimation and repression. The latter is a defense that leads to neurosis because the impulse and the ideas associated with it are denied access to consciousness. The former, on the other hand, is a "successful defence"; that is, sublimation is, like repression, a prophylactic mechanism, but a mechanism that involves a substantial release of the energy contained in the original impulse. This can occur because the impulse is redirected to *socially acceptable ends*. As Freud wrote in 1917:

> There are in general very many ways of tolerating deprivation of libidinal satisfaction without falling ill as a result. . . . Among

[11] Ibid., 74.

[12] Freud usually talks about sublimation not as a change of object, but only as a change in aim. However, he does include a change in object when he mentions sublimation in *The New Introductory Lectures on Psycho-Analysis*, SE, xxii, 97.

[13] This is similar to the way Freud says dream thoughts enter consciousness and the way a repressed impulse may in part be released by associative ideas.

these protective processes against falling ill owing to deprivation there is one which has gained special cultural significance. It consists in the sexual trend abandoning its aim of obtaining a component or a reproductive pleasure and taking on another which is related genetically to the abandoned one but is no longer sexual and must be described as social. We call this process 'sublimation,' in accordance with the general estimate that places social aims higher than the sexual ones, which are at bottom self-interested.[14]

It will soon become clear that this "general estimate" has neglected to investigate the sacrifice that the individual makes in redirecting his sexual aims and the cummulative effect that this sacrifice has on civilization.

The price sublimation demands of the individual is especially clear in the study of Leonardo. The satisfaction of the sexual instincts does not occur sexually; gratification is the pale shadow of the intensity of the original desire.[15] Leonardo's intense search for a father, combined with his longing to remain an infant with a mother, is channeled into the attempt to know scientifically the object of his love. As Freud notes: "The postponement of loving until full knowledge is acquired ends in a substitution of the latter for the former. A man who has won his way to a state of knowledge cannot properly be said to love and hate; he remains beyond love and hatred. He has investigated instead of loving."[16] Leonardo, in his contemplation of the world and its forces, removes himself from relationships in the world. For us, there is what remains of the man, his contributions to civilization. Freud seems to tell us that these remains were all that Leonardo was in his own time. His investigations replaced his desire; his works became the totality of his being in the world.

---

[14] *Introductory Lectures on Psycho-Analysis*, SE, XVI, 345.

[15] See Norman O. Brown, *Life against Death: The Psychoanalytical Meaning of History* (Middletown, Conn., 1959), 169, where he refers to sublimations as "symbols of symbols." Brown's critical explication of Freud's concept of sublimation is as intelligent and perceptive as his "way out" of sublimation is alternately simpleminded and mysterious.

[16] *Leonardo*, SE, XI, 75.

Of course, the argument here is not that Leonardo should have acted out his sexual desires instead of making art. Such an argument would not only be wrongheaded, it would be outside a theory of history, since it would be an attempt to stipulate how Leonardo *ought* to have acted, rather than to *interpret* what in fact he did do. The question being opened here concerns the person's (here, Leonardo's) awareness of his sacrifice; what self-consciousness of the "costs of production" in contributing to civilization is possible? From Freud's analysis of Leonardo, it is clear that the artist was unaware of this cost. Norman O. Brown's remarks about sublimation generally in *Life against Death* apply quite accurately to the life of Leonardo. "Sublimation," Brown writes, "is the search for lost life; it presupposes and perpetuates the loss of life and cannot be the mode in which life itself is lived. Sublimation is the mode of an organism which must discover life rather than live, must know rather than be."[17]

Sublimation, then, is a particularly paradoxical concept in Freud's work. On the one hand, it is the successful defense par excellence—the mechanism to which we owe the greatest achievements in the history of civilization. On the other hand, sublimation is the mode that leaves the person denied, sacrificing happiness for creation without acknowledging the cost involved.[18] When one grasps the dynamic of sublimation, the pessimism in Freud's stated therapeutic aim, "to transform hysterical misery into common unhappiness," becomes most meaningful. If sublimation is a defense that incorporates socially sanctioned satisfaction, we must remember that it is the sanction and not the satisfaction that sets this defense apart from others. That is, all defenses—even symptoms—entail some satisfaction, even as they all entail various levels of repression.[19] Sublimation is a "successful"

[17] *Life against Death*, 171.

[18] I am leaving aside the question of self-conscious sublimation, since this is not what Freud is talking about in *Leonardo*. Sublimation as a result of analysis emerges out of the transference, and this is discussed at length below.

[19] On "satisfactions," see Lacan, *The Four Fundamental Concepts of Psycho-Analysis*, trans. Alan Sheridan (New York, 1977), 165–168.

defense because through it desire confirms dominant social values. This process of confirmation is often seen in social or historical terms as progress, but this social perspective may be blind to the repression that has us view progress as the reaffirmation of values without attention to the costs of the deflection of desire.

Thus, Freud's distinction between the concepts of repression and sublimation should not obscure the limitations of the latter process, limitations that contributed greatly to his therapeutic pessimism. We have already seen in regard to Leonardo the problem of the residue of the original impulse that is left behind in the unconscious. The distinction between repression and sublimation lies in the difference in the amount of libido that can be released; a distinction in degree and not in kind. This fits in quite well with another line of Freud's thought: that there is only a conventional distinction between the abnormal and the normal person.

An escape from neurosis through sublimation is available only to a minority. Freud, of course, did not as a result view the majority of people as neurotics. There are other successful defenses, and society is able to tolerate persons engaging in a variety of pathological activities without finding it necessary to label those persons neurotic. In other words, there are those who do not sublimate and who have their "pathologies," *but who remain socially functional*, which I take to be one of Freud's major criteria for normality.[20] As the study of the nature of unconscious desire presented above made clear, however, such persons remain fundamentally denied, perhaps even in profound pain.

Sublimation is essentially a social mode of psychic defense which leaves the person ungratified. The concept of sublimation, then, leads to the question of the person's relationship to civilization—to the status of desire in the social realm.

---

[20] Of course, Freud's concept of normality rests on "the abnormal" and is not divorced from it. Functional here simply means the ability to love and work. See *An Outline of Psycho-Analysis, SE*, xvii, 195, and Jürgen Habermas, *Knowledge and Human Interests*, trans. Jeremy J. Shapiro (Boston, 1971), 274.

Freud seems clear on this point, maintaining that a deep sacrifice is being made when the individual joins any group. "This replacement of the power of the individual by the power of a community constitutes the decisive step of civilization," he writes in *Civilization and Its Discontents*. "The essence of it lies in the fact that the members of the community restrict themselves in their possibilities of satisfaction, whereas the individual knew no such restrictions."[21] In Freud's description of the first community of human beings in *Totem and Taboo* (1913), the deferred obedience to the murdered father from the sons who killed him is seen as a sublimation of oedipal desires:

> what had up to then been prevented by his [the father's] actual existence was thence-forward prohibited by the sons themselves, in accordance with the psychological procedure so familiar to us in psycho-analysis under the name of "deferred obedience." They revoked their deed by forbidding the killing of the totem, the substitute for their father; and they renounced its fruits by resigning their claim to the women who had now been set free.[22]

Here is a clear case in which sublimation is an agreed-upon repression. If the founding sublimation of civilization is a general mediation—if not denial—of desire, Freud suggests that civilization can not only incorporate a necessary degree of repression, but can itself become an important source of frustration, anxiety, and pathology.

Given this connection among civilization, repression, and sublimation, the link between this last concept and "progress" takes on new meaning. The denial that created society after the killing of the primal father left its residue of impulses in the unconscious. This denial is repeated in every generation, and as the civilization grows, denial, too, grows. As people are able, they sublimate their impulses into socially acceptable acts, what is acceptable itself being defined

---

[21] *SE*, xxi, 95. See also below, Chapter 5.
[22] *SE*, xiii, 143.

by the general level of the group's defenses. Thus, those who sublimate have their own possibilities of satisfactions limited by the level of the group's denial, but their activity is an attempt to escape the pain of this denial by redirecting their desires so that in another form they can be gratified. This cycle of duplicity takes its toll on humanity. As Freud notes in *Civilization and Its Discontents:*

> . . . it is impossible to overlook the extent to which civilization is built up upon a renunciation of instinct, how much it presupposes precisely the nonsatisfaction (by suppression, repression or some other means?) of powerful instincts. This "cultural frustration" dominates the large field of social relationships between human beings. As we already know, it is the cause of the hostility against which all civilizations have to struggle.[23]

For Freud, society becomes a source of suffering because of the very process through which it attempts to protect the individual from suffering. But the point here is not that we would be better off without any repression; the point is not simply to urge more satisfaction and less protection. Freud does not dismiss the importance of the prophylactic function of society. Society's dual nature stems from its foundation in the oedipal structure of infantile sexuality. That is, there is a profound conflict of desire at the roots of society— its protective function stems from desire as does the attempt to escape that function. The conflict can no more be eliminated than can the role of the father in the oedipal triangle. In recognizing the repressive aspects of the social defense, sublimation, we cannot forget that society is a result, as well as an inhibitor, of desire.

Freud regarded with scorn the idea that the problems concerning the satisfaction of desire stemmed solely from society because this notion was blind to the individual's ambivalence in the group. Society, Freud says, embodies the

---

[23] *SE*, xxi, 97.

protective devices that we would use (and do use) as individuals:

> This contention holds that what we call our civilization is largely responsible for our misery, and that we should be much happier if we gave it up and returned to primitive conditions. I call this contention astonishing because, in whatever way we may define the concept of civilization, it is a certain fact that all the things with which we seek to protect ourselves against the threats that emanate from the sources of suffering are part of that very civilization.[24]

Many post-Freudian thinkers have seen that contemporary society has turned increasingly from providing protection for the individual to becoming the chief source of suffering. Recognizing that the repressive component of sublimation may be, in Herbert Marcuse's phrase, a "surplus repression," and fearing that this surplus is one of the major sources of social aggressiveness and violence, they have attempted to find some form of social satisfaction—a reasonable happiness—that would not be a dangerous form of desexualization. I shall discuss some of these attempts in detail in the next chapter, but here it must be underlined that Freud consistently rejected any way out of the individual's ambivalent connection with society, since this connection emerged from the very structure of desire.

Freud does not offer any resolution of ambivalence, and given was shown in Section I—that psycho-analysis is first and foremost a historical science—it is easy to see why. Psycho-analysis cannot propose anything for the future; it is concerned with the creation of a consciousness that *can* negate—that can move to the future based on an understanding of the past. To forget that ambivalence results from a conflict of desire is not to resolve the contradiction, the conflict, that leads to the process of sublimation. To suppose that one can choose one of the conflicting desires without cost, without struggle, is to have learned nothing from Freud's

[24] Ibid., 86.

study of the unconscious. Psycho-analysis is an attempt to
uncover the meaning of the ambivalence, the cost of the resolution of conflict.[25] The meaning is apprehended by the
analysand through the transference phenomenon. When the
analysand apprehends this meaning, the treatment is over
and self-conscious action may begin. When the analysis reveals profound contradictions between the desires of the individual and the potential for gratification in the group as it
stands, the possibility for free, self-conscious radical action
exists.[26]

The two senses of sublimation that Laplanche and Pontalis
spoke of have played a role throughout this discussion of the
concept. The connection of sublimation to the great works
of civilization has been noted repeatedly, and we know that
the value that society places on the results of the process
can be extraordinary. Sublimation is the psychic stuff of the
ideology of progress. Civilization progresses through sublimation; the mechanism perhaps can be called the liberal defense (or even the defense of liberalism). The second sense
of sublimation, which concerned the dynamics of the transformation, revealed the darker side of the process. By contributing to the growth of civilization, sublimation contributed to the increased denial necessary to maintain that
civilization.

The concept of the transference is used to describe the
relationship that arises between the analyst and the analysand, in which the infantile feelings of the latter are redirected onto the former. For example, the analysand may act
or feel, or both, toward the psycho-analyst as he would toward

[25] For an interesting account of the nature of paradox in philosophy and
ambivalence in psycho-analysis, see John Wisdom, "Philosophy and Psycho-Analysis," in his *Philosophy and Psycho-Analysis* (Oxford, 1953), 169–
181.
[26] Of course, radical activity is not the only way in which to react to profound contradictions: *Civilization and Its Discontents*, SE, xxi, 84. The revelation of these contradictions, however, itself can be part of a radical project. See, for example, Joel Kovel, *The Age of Desire: Case Studied of a Radical
Psychoanalyst* (New York, 1981).

his father, so that it seems as if these feelings are transferred from father to "doctor."[27] This relationship does not only occur in the analytic situation, but it is seen there most clearly. In the pages that follow I will explicate Freud's views on the phenomena of the transference and show that the structure of this relationship is the crucial starting point from which psycho-analysis can move from the individual to the group. We shall see in the following chapter in what sense the "transference," as a basis for the psycho-analytic apprehension of group phenomena, has radical political implications. Attention to this political dimension will involve a broadening of the concept of the transference that is found in Freud's writings, but I regard this broadening as a development of the original concept that is supported by the corpus as a whole when read as a theory of history.

One of the most famous patients in the history of psychoanalysis, the woman who initiated the "talking cure," is Anna O. In her relationship with the physician Joseph Breuer one sees a clear example of the transference. As Ernest Jones relates the story, Breuer broke off the treatment as a result of the complaints of his wife. When Anna was told of her doctor's decision, she severely regressed from what had become a fairly healthy state:

> He announced this [his decision] to Anna O., who was by now much better, and bade her good-by. But that evening he was fetched back to find her in a greatly excited state, apparently as ill as ever. The patient, who according to him had appeared to be an asexual being and had never made any allusion to such a forbidden topic throughout the treatment, was now in the throes of an hysterical childbirth (psychocyesis), the logical termination of a phantom pregnancy that had been developing in response to Breuer's ministrations.[28]

---

[27] I put the word "doctor," and will put the word "patient," in quotation marks to convey my view that the medical model is not a necessary component of psycho-analysis. In the discussion of contemporary professional psychoanalysis below, these quotation marks are dropped.

[28] Ernest Jones, *The Life and Work of Sigmund Freud*, vol. 1 (New York, 1953), 224–225. See also Freud and Joseph Breuer, *Studies on Hysteria*, SE, 11, 21–48.

Anna O.'s phantom pregnancy had a great effect on Breuer and his colleague Freud. The latter began to investigate the sexual content of the relationship between "doctor" and "patient," which seemed to parallel the dynamics of the formation of neuroses. Twenty years after the incident between Breuer and Anna O., Freud commented on the psycho-analytic approach to the transference: "The fact of the emergence of the transference in its crudely sexual form, whether affectionate or hostile, in every treatment of neurosis, although this is neither desired nor induced by either doctor or patient, has always seemed to me the most irrefragable proof that the source of the driving forces of neurosis lies in sexual life."[29]

In analysis, the transference emerges first as part of the resistance to uncovering the unconscious. That is, the analysand uses his feelings for the analyst to block the penetration of the interpretation into sensitive areas. Freud emphasizes in an essay of 1912, however, that this peculiar relationship between "doctor" and "patient" is not confined to the analytic setting, but emerges from any treatment of neurosis. "It is not a fact that transference emerges with greater intensity and lack of restraint during psycho-analysis than outside it," he writes. "In institutions where nervous patients are treated non-analytically, we can observe transference occurring with the greatest intensity and in the most unworthy forms, extending to nothing less than mental bondage, and moreover showing the plainest erotic colouring."[30] Psychoanalysis is distinguished from these other treatments in that it deliberately uses the phenomena of transference to further the aims of the treatment.

The task of the analyst at the early stages of treatment is "to convert dangers into gains"—to enable the analysand to recognize that the unconscious infantile impulses which the treatment is trying to discover are being manifested in the way he relates to the analyst in the present. Freud sees the

[29] *On the History of the Psycho-Analytic Movement, SE,* xiv, 12.
[30] "The Dynamics of Transference," *SE,* xii, 101.

analyst as struggling against the analysand's tendency to resort to modes of distortion provided by unconscious processes (the dreamwork) and against hostile impulses that are being directed onto him from the analysand.[31]

Freud distinguishes between two types of transference, the positive, made up of affectionate feelings, and the negative, made up of hostile feelings. Both these poles can be used in the service of the resistance, although the latter type is particularly damaging to the success of the treatment. In either case the analyst should make use of these feelings in the search for meaning, and not deny their existence or merely avoid them:

> To urge the patient to suppress, renounce or sublimate her instincts the moment she has admitted her erotic transference would be, not an analytic way of dealing with them, but a senseless one. It would be just as though, after summoning up a spirit from the underworld by cunning spells, one were to send him down again without having asked him a single question. One would have brought the repressed into consciousness, only to repress it once more in a fright.[32]

This passage reveals the essential function of the transference in the course of analysis. The infantile impulses are called up from the unconscious to defend against the treatment. Since the impulses are present in the analytic session itself— since they are immediately audible to the analysand in his own discourse—the development of the conflicts may well be explained by the forces that were activated to camouflage this development. In the relationship of analyst and analysand the constructions of the latter's past become activated in the present without the mediation of repression or the dreamwork. The history of the analysand is revealed through interpretation of the "patient's" reports of the past, dreams, and the exhibition of that past to both persons in the present. In his *Discours de Rome*, Jacques Lacan described the

---

[31] Ibid., 103, 105.
[32] "Observations on Transference Love," *SE*, xii, 164.

transference phenomenon in analysis as follows: "For in this labor which he [analysand] undertakes to reconstruct this construct for *another*, he finds again the fundamental alienation which made him construct it *like another one*, and which has always destined it to be stripped from him *by another*."[33] The analysand's constructions (symptoms or pathological activity) are imitated, reconstructed, in analysis, and in the manifest infantile roots of this imitation he sees the profound self-estrangement that is at the basis of his being in the world. The guise is stripped from the constructs to reveal the history of misrepresentations that were required to protect the analysand from himself, from his desire.

The reordering of the analysand's past through the meaning found in the discourse of the analytic situation is the essence of psycho-analytic procedure. In his last book, *An Outline of Psycho-Analysis*, Freud described the kinds of relationships that were created in the transference:

> The patient is not satisfied with regarding the analyst in the light of reality as a helper and advisor who, moreover, is remunerated for the trouble he takes and who would be content with some such role as that of a guide on a difficult mountain climb. On the contrary, the patient sees in him the return, the reincarnation, of some important figure out of his childhood or past, and consequently transfers on to him feelings and reactions which undoubtedly applied to this prototype. This fact of transference soon proves to be a factor of undreamt-of importance, on the one hand an instrument of irreplaceable value and on the other hand a source of serious dangers.[34]

The important figures from the past will usually be the parents. The nature of their importance indicates immediately that the analysand's feelings will be ambivalent. The analyst must try to cultivate the positive aspect of the transference, and often the "patient" will work for his own recovery to

[33] Jacques Lacan, "the Function of Language in Psychoanalysis," in *The Language of the Self*, trans. Anthony Wilden (New York, 1968), 11.
[34] *SE*, xxiii, 174–175.

please the analyst and to satisfy an infantile longing to please the parent. Positive transference, Freud wrote of this particular twist of events, "alters the whole analytic situation; it pushes to one side the patient's rational aim of becoming healthy and free from ailments. Instead of it there emerges the aim of pleasing the analyst and winning his applause and love."[35]

This ironic reversal, in which a resistance to the treatment begins to complement the analyst's efforts, also seems to jeopardize the reading of Freud that has thus far been presented. I have repeatedly stressed that in psycho-analysis interpretation is carried out, for the most part, by the analysand. If the task of interpretation is his, however, his independence seems crucial in the search for meaning. The transference relationship appears to be a great threat to that independence.[36]

Freud is well aware of the dangers inherent in this "positive" transference relationship. He recognizes that a "false cure" may arise out of a wish to please the analyst. Such a "cure" would involve the disappearance of the original symptoms, but only at the price of a severe dependence of the "patient" on the analyst. Freud emphatically states that "psycho-analytic treatment is founded on truthfulness";[37] the analyst must not merely recapitulate the role played by the neurotic's parents, but must penetrate this role and reveal its meaning. He warns the analyst about the dangers of the influence which the transference phenomenon creates for the treatment: "However much the analyst may be tempted to

---

[35] Ibid., 175.

[36] This "threat to independence" is often talked about as "suggestion," both by Freud and in commentaries on his work. The "problem of suggestion" is extremely important to those who are concerned with the epistemological "foundations" of psycho-analysis. A central text of Freud's in this regard is Lecture xxvii, "Transference," of *Introductory Lectures on Psycho-Analysis* (1917). The philosopher of science Adolf Grünbaum has written repeatedly on the problem of suggestion for the clinical testing of psychoanalysis. See, for example, *The Foundations of Psychoanalysis* (Berkeley, 1984).

[37] *An Outline of Psycho-Analysis*, SE, xxiii, 175. See also "Analysis Terminable and Interminable," *SE*, xxiii, 248.

become a teacher, model and ideal for other people and to create men in his own image, he should not forget that that is not his task in the analytic relationship, and indeed that he will be disloyal to his task if he allows himself to be led on by his inclinations."[38] Above all, the analyst must always ensure that the "patient" keep in mind that they are in an analytic situation—that their relationship is based upon their attempt to discover the meaning of the analysand's history.[39] The transference is a tool used to understand the past that is contained in the present; it is not in any way a "natural" or "normal" relationship. Freud is clear in his account of the transference as an artificial construction, an "intermediate region between illness and real life."[40] The transference relationship is a neurotic relationship, but a neurosis that is contained by the analytic situation itself: "The danger of these states of transference evidently lies in the patient's misunderstanding of their nature and taking them for fresh real experiences instead of reflections of the past . . ." Freud wrote in *An Outline of Psycho-Analysis*. "It is the analyst's task constantly to tear the patient out of his menacing illusion and to show him again and again that what he takes to be new

[38] *An Outline of Psycho-Analysis*, SE, xxiii, 175.

[39] Jung accuses Freud of avoiding the transference in that psycho-analysis keeps the relationship contrived, specific to the treatment. Jung regards that transference as a "natural phenomenon," much like the relationship between a woman and her clergyman, the general practitioner and the husband (these examples are from C. G. Jung, *The Psychology of the Transference*, trans. R. F. C. Hull [Princeton, 1966], 8). Both doctor and patient are changed during their interaction, Jung believes, and there is no reason for their relationship not to continue outside of the treatment. On the contrary, he feels, extension of the transference outside of the analysis reflects the naturalness of the analytic dialogue. Psycho-analysis, however, regards the transference as an induced neurosis. The important similarities between Jung on transference and Ferenczi's later ideas of therapy, and further similarities with the ideas of contemporary analysts who emphasize "positive therapeutic experiences," should not obscure the fact that Freud regarded the type of influence that analytical (Jungian) psychology encourages the doctor to have as a form of "mental bondage." On the influence that Ferenczi's views on therapy had on the neo-Freudians, see Russell Jacoby, *The Repression of Psychoanalysis: Otto Fenichel and the Political Freudians* (New York, 1983), 108–109.

[40] "Remembering, Repeating and Working Through," SE, xii, 154.

117

real life is a reflection of the past."[41] Like a neurosis, then, the transference is a reflection of the past, but unlike the pathology, it is also a reflection on the past. The analytic situation enables the analysand to know, and not merely to repeat.[42]

The role of the transference is to bring analysis to an end.[43] The relationship between the two persons in the treatment manifests the meaning of the analysand's history in an immediate form. Freud denies the analyst the role of prediction in this situation; that is to say, he denies the analyst the role of planning the future for his "patient." Such planning has no basis in psycho-analytic theory, which, as was shown in considerable detail above, is a theory of history—a framework for making meaning of the past. Psycho-analysis ends with the relative completion of the self-consciousness of the person, "*Wo Es war, soll Ich werden.*"[44] Freud's famous dic-

---

[41] *SE*, xxiii, 176–177.

[42] It is with the concept of the transference that the most crucial epistemological issues arise for psycho-analysis. The psycho-analytic treatment of the transference is, in part, intended to address the problem of suggestion in the analytic session: that is, the problem of the analyst leading the analysand through interpretations and associations that the latter would not develop in any other context, and that do not correspond to the past "as it really was." It should be clear from my explication of "transference" that I do not see Freud as having *removed* suggestion from the analytic session, but rather as having made suggestion itself subject to analysis. If one is looking for an epistemological *foundation* for psycho-analysis—if one is looking for a way out of, a ground for, the hermeneutic circle—this move will clearly not be satisfactory. However, the search for foundations, as much of contemporary philosophy and literary criticism has been saying, may be more of a symptom of the misdirection of epistemology than it is a telling dilemma for psycho-analysis. Donald P. Spence's *Narrative Truth and Historical Truth: Meaning and Interpretation in Psychoanalysis* (New York, 1982) confronts this issue from the perspective of a practicing psychoanalyst.

[43] The essay in which Freud deals with the end of analysis at great length is "Analysis Terminable and Interminable," *SE*, xxiii, 209–252.

[44] Translated by the *Standard Edition* as "where id was, there ego shall be," *New Introductory Lectures on Psycho-Analysis*, *SE*, xxii, 80. Lacan, in "The Freudian Thing, or the Meaning of the Return to Freud in Psychoanalysis" (*Ecrits*, 128–129), presents an extended rendering of the phrase; and, in "The Agency of the Letter in the Unconscious or Reason since Freud" (*Ecrits*, 171), he offers a shorter translation: "I must come to be where that was."

118

tum does not point to anything like a "total personality," nor does it describe what was later to be called "self-actualization."[45] The unconscious does not disappear when the last check arrives at the analyst's office. But if the treatment is successful, the unconscious can be read; with interpretation, its signs can begin to be known. This knowing, this self-consciousness, is the *freedom* of psycho-analysis; freedom that comes from the struggle with the unconscious (its signs) through the transference, and as the *negation* of the transference. If there is to be any freedom, the transference must also be worked through and finally negated. Freud is emphatic about the necessity for the end of the transference, and it is crucial for him *that the final object of analysis is freedom*:

> Perhaps it [the outcome of the treatment] may depend too, on whether the personality of the analyst allows of the patient's putting him in the place of his ego ideal, and this involves a temptation for the analyst to play the part of prophet, savior and redeemer to the patient. Since the rules of analysis are diametrically opposed to the physician's making use of his personality in any such manner, it must be honestly confessed that here we have another limitation to the effectiveness of analysis; after all, analysis does not set out to make pathological reactions impossible, but to give the patient's ego *freedom* to decide one way or the other.[46]

It is with this freedom to decide one way or the other that psycho-analysis ends and, in some sense, where this reading of Freud must also end. That is, the interpretation of the past ends for Freud in the freedom of the present; speculations on the future are extra-psycho-analytic. However, the psycho-analytic concept of freedom must still be articulated more

[45] The term "total personality" occurs in Benjamin B. Wolman, *The Unconscious Mind: The Meaning of Freudian Psychology* (Englewood Cliffs, N.J., 1968), 82. The term "self-actualization" is Abraham Maslow's; see, for example Maslow, *Toward a Psychology of Being*, 2d ed. (New York, 1968), 133–145.
[46] *The Ego and the Id, SE*, xix, 50n.

119

fully if the political implications of psycho-analysis and especially of the transference are to be understood.

Although I have avoided any extended discussion of post-Freudian psychoanalysis in this book, the topic of transference calls for some remarks on the ways in which my own reading of Freud cuts across some of the contemporary debates within *professional* psychoanalysis. These remarks are not meant to provide insight into the clinical or theoretical concerns of contemporary analysts, *except* insofar as they help to clarify Freud's project more fully. As Russell Jacoby has shown in some detail,[47] psychoanalysis after Freud, particularly in America, has shrunk from its original form of cultural criticism to an increasingly marginal medical discourse. Despite this fact, the questions of history, negation, and freedom that are readily found in Freud's writings can also be discovered in the works of some of his followers.

As Roy Schafer has noted, the "progress of the discipline of psychoanalysis is expressed perhaps most obviously in its theory of transference and the therapeutic effects of the interpretation of transference."[48] A major theoretical development and a clinical exigency have greatly altered the classical concept of transference, which we have examined thus far. The increasing attention to object relations theory, and the demand that the therapist provide some positive emotional experience have led to some major changes in the theoretical understanding of the patient/analyst relationship. Although I do not intend to discuss the vast literature on these two closely related subjects in any detail, as we see what is at stake in these developments we shall understand more fully Freud's "transference" as the negation of a past that can lead to a new acknowledging of history through freedom.

The term "object relations," much like the word "instinct,"

---

[47] *The Repression of Psychoanalysis*, passim. See also Henry Abelove, "Freud, Male Homosexuality, and the Americans," *Dissent*, 33 (Winter 1986), 59–69.

[48] Schafer, "The Interpretation of Transference and the Conditions for Loving," *Journal of the American Psychoanalytic Association*, 25 (1977), 335; reprinted in *The Analytic Attitude* (New York, 1983).

has different meanings within various psychoanalytic schools of thought. There is, however a general signification, and two analysts have expressed it as follows: "The term . . . designates theories, or aspects of theories, concerned with exploring the relationship between real, external people and internal images and residues of relations with them, and the significance of these residues for psychic functioning. Approaches to these problems constitute the major focus of psychoanalytic theorizing over the past several decades."[49] All object relations theories emphasize the fact that from the start of life, the human being is enmeshed in relationships with others. Many of the theories, particularly those of Melanie Klein and the analysts influenced by her, stress the very early connections made between the infant and its surroundings. In this view the Oedipus complex does not mark the transition from the individual to the social; here, the individual is always already a social being.

The theoretical focus on the very early stages of development has been paralleled by a clinical emphasis on character or personality disorders, the origins of which are said to be very early in the infant's evolution. The treatment of these disorders has lead to changes in the technique of therapy, changes that bear in important ways on the idea of and clinical use of the transference. In brief, if the analysand suffering from a narcissistic personality disorder does not even have the minimum ego structure for entering into a transference relationship at the start of analysis, some technique for building this structure has to become part of the analytic process.[50] But how do you build an ego structure without

---

[49] Jay R. Greenberg and Stephen A. Mitchell, *Object Relations in Psychoanalytic Theory* (Cambridge, 1983), 12. Greenberg and Mitchell use a very broad designation for "object relations" and defend this designation in their first chapter.

[50] There is a vast literature on the problem of a "minimum ego structure" for transference. See, for example, Victor Calef's introduction and conclusion to an APA panel discussion on the transference, "On The Current Concept of the Transference Neurosis," *Journal of the American Psychoanalytic Association*, 19 (1971), 22–25, 89–97; Lawrence Friedman, "The Therapeutic Alliance," *IJP*, 50 (1969), 139–153; Merton Gill, "The Analysis of the Transfer-

playing the role of a "teacher, model, and ideal" which Freud specifically warned against?

This question has animated much psychoanalytic discussion since the 1950s, when the issues of "positive therapeutic effect" and the "corrective emotional experience" in therapy became hot subjects of debate. I do not intend to summarize that debate here, but it should be clear that the understanding of psycho-analysis as a theory of history disallows any attempt to make therapy an arena for development, in contradistinction to being that field in which development—or the lack of it—can be understood.[51]

I have said that the analytic transference is a neurotic form of repetition that makes possible acknowledgement of the past and thus its overcoming in a dialectical negation. Contemporary psychoanalysis has wrestled with trying to define more exactly the relations between present and past within the transference, and the status of analytic interpretation in making a connection between them. Like most problems in psychoanalysis, this one has not been only a philosophical question, but has taken on urgency due to the changes in the therapeutic status of the transference just mentioned. That is, as analysis has taken on cases deemed incapable of transference, the analyst has played a more active role. This new

ence," *Journal of the American Psychoanalytic Association,* 27 (1979), 263–288; Greenberg and Mitchell, *Object Relations in Psychoanalytic Theory,* 388–398; Heinz Kohut, "The Psychoanalytic Treatment of Narcissistic Personality Disorders: Outline of a Systematic Approach," *Psychoanalytic Study of the Child,* 23 (1968), 86–133; Nathan Leites, *Interpreting Transference* New York, (1979); Hans W. Loewald, "The Transference Neurosis: Comments on the Concept and the Phenomenon," *Journal of the American Psychoanalytic Association,* 19 (1971), 54–66; Benjamin Wolstein, *Transference: Its Structure and Function in Psychoanalytic Therapy,* 2d ed. (New York, 1964); Elizabeth R. Zetzel, "Current Concepts of Transference," *IJP,* 37 (1956), 369–375; François Roustang, *Dire Mastery: Discipleship from Freud to Lacan,* trans. Ned Lukacher (Baltimore, 1982); and Roustang, *Psychoanalysis Never Lets Go,* trans. Ned Lukacher (Baltimore, 1983).

[51] The important clinical question about those patients who are incapable of a transference of any kind cannot be treated here. It should be obvious, however, from even a cursory glance at Freud's writings and the available evidence in regard to therapeutic efficacy, that psychoanalysis is unsuitable for some patients.

role—or, this role conceptualized in a new way—has raised questions about whether the "past" called up by psychoanalysis is merely a story conjured up in the treatment situation.

These questions are particularly interesting from our perspective insofar as they dovetail very neatly with questions raised in contemporary philosophy of history. At least since Hegel, philosophy of history has been concerned with defining exactly in what way the past is determined by the present. More recent philosophers and historians, from R. G. Collingwood to Hayden White, have seen the presentistic aspects of all historical inquiry not as an evil to be minimized in the pursuit of a notion of objectivity taken from other disciplines, but as the very substance of historical knowing.[52]

Similarly, the "presentistic" aspects of the analytic situation have received increasing attention since Freud's time.[53] For many analysts and theorists, the "felt acceptance" of interpretations is much more important than the accuracy of "historic" reconstructions. The transference, I have said, is a repetition, a re-surgence of infantile impulses in a controlled environment. This does not mean that the task of analysis is to recover the origins of these repetitions; to go back to some state before desire became mediated by ambivalence. This idea is pre-Freudian—characteristic of Freud himself, of course, before his break with the seduction theory and remaining a tendency in his work insofar as the seduction theory was never fully abandoned. Rather than bringing the analysand back to his past, the transference allows him to see more clearly the patterns of the past in the present. It

[52] The literature on the role of the present in the writing of history is enormous. See, for example, R. G. Collingwood, *The Idea of History* (Oxford, 1946); Hayden V. White, *Metahistory: The Historical Imagination in Nineteenth Century Europe* (Baltimore, 1978); *Metahistory: Six Critiques, History and Theory*, Beiheft 19 (1980); Michael S. Roth, "Foucault's 'History of the Present'," *History and Theory*, 20 (1981), 32–46.

[53] See, for example, Roy Schafer, "Narration in Psychoanalytic Dialogue," in *On Narrative*, ed. W. J. T. Mitchell (Chicago, 1981), 48–49; and "The Psychoanalytic Life History," in his *Language and Insight* (New Haven, 1978), 3–27.

123

should be clear that this notion of making sense of the past in the present does not rely on some notion of the essential continuity of change over time. The psycho-analytic theory of making meaning of memory assumes nothing of the kind, but it neither assumes nor celebrates an essential discontinuity. Too, the idea of "making meaning" does not project some transcendental guarantee or stable signification. On the contrary, it emphasizes that meanings generated through the psycho-analytic theory of history are the product of a always already changing present in confrontation with a significant past that shifts in relation to this present.

Thus, the transference is not a technique to achieve on a personal level the goal of a Rankean history as it really happened. It is instead the enactment of the past in the present in the service of discovering historical meaning and direction; of making meaning out of the directionality one discovers in constructing and reconstructing one's life. In other words, the transference brings together what Donald Spence has called "narrative truth" with "historical truth."[54] The transference is the vehicle for creating meaning and direction out of a life that has lost significant connections between past, present, and future. Constructing with and through analysis the narrative that will make these connections can be what Roy Schafer calls "experiencing the past for the first time";[55] by giving meaning and direction to the past in the present, it is the actualization of psycho-analysis as a theory of history.

Freud's understanding of the transference points toward the piecing together of a history out of the ruins of the past. It is a reflexive process; a process that continually acknowledges its own construction so as to reveal the traps of repetition. The self-conscious development of a history one can live with—or the development of self-consciousness through

---

[54] Donald P. Spence, *Narrative Truth and Historical Truth: Meaning and Interpretation in Psychoanalysis* (New York, 1982). See also Serge Viderman, *La construction de l'espace analytique* (Paris, 1970).

[55] "The Interpretation of Transference," 359.

a reappropriation of one's history—reveals the psycho-analytic concept of freedom.

In order to make clearer the freedom that results from the transference phenomenon, I believe it is most helpful to turn to the philosophy of Hegel. I do so for this specific purpose only, with no intention of comparing or contrasting Hegel's thought with Freud's, or considering the question of his influence on Freud.[56] The substance of mind, Hegel tells the reader, is freedom.[57] Freedom, for Hegel, is an absence of dependence on the Other, but this independence can be won only through the Other, by overcoming the Other. Free mind is mind "at home with itself," but not mind without division or contradiction. As Hegel explains in *The Philosophy of Mind*: "even in its extreme disunity, in this violent detachment of itself from the root of its intrinsically ethical nature, in this complete self-contradiction, mind yet remains identical with itself and therefore free."[58] For Hegel, as for Freud, *the* mind preserving itself in contradiction is in pain. The psycho-analytic investigation of the contradiction of "knowing yet not knowing" is an investigation of a mind in pain and an attempt to understand that pain. The mind in this immediate (unreflective) state of contradiction is free only implicitly, according to Hegel.[59] The reading of Freud that has been presented here has no difficulty with this notion.

[56] Many writers have investigated the links between the thought of Hegel and Freud, although not in any systematic form. The influence of Hegel and the mystical tradition on which Hegel drew on Norman O. Brown's writings about psycho-analysis is great. Herbert Marcuse, in *Eros and Civilization: A Philosophical Inquiry into Freud* (Boston, 1955), 106–126, makes use of the *Phenomenology of Spirit* in his reading of Freud. Paul Ricoeur, *Freud and Philosophy: An Essay on Interpretation*, trans. Denis Savage (New Haven, 1970), 459–470, also makes use of the *Phenomenology of Spirit*. The influence of Hegel—through his interpreter, Alexandre Kojève—on Lacan's reading of Freud is fundamental. See also the texts of Jean Hyppolite (including an exchange with Lacan) on Freud in *Figures de la pensée philosophique* (Paris, 1971), 373–442.

[57] *The Philosophy of Mind*, trans. W. Wallace and A. V. Miller (Oxford, 1971), 15.

[58] Ibid.

[59] Ibid., 16.

Hegel sees the journey of mind to actual freedom as the journey from subjectivity (in which mind is trying to understand itself as itself) through objectivity (where the freedom of mind is objectified in an external relation such as property) to Absolute Mind (mind as art, religion, and philosophy). It is clear that when Hegel writes about mind he is not usually referring to what Freud was signifying by the same word. Absolute Mind, for example, is not concerned with the minds of artists, religious men, and philosophers, but with art, religion, and philosophy. However, in the second section of *The Philosophy of Mind*, "Subjective Mind," Hegel turns to psychology, and one can see the similarity between his and Freud's views of *the* mind.

Hegel discusses the nature of psychology in terms of what the discipline posits as the end (in the sense of final cause) of mind. He sees the end of the mind as a liberation from its immediacy, a liberation that enables it to look upon itself, to be conscious of itself, and to be free. He writes about the discipline of psychology generally and the need to remain conscious of the end of the activities of mind:

> That [true aim of mind] can only be the intelligible unity of mind, and its activity can only have itself as aim; i.e., its aim can only be to get rid of the form of immediacy or subjectivity, to reach and get hold of itself, and to liberate itself to itself. In this way the so-called faculties of mind as thus distinguished are only to be treated as steps of this liberation. And this is the only *rational* mode of studying the mind and its various activities.[60]

The end of mind for Hegel is freedom; the goal of psychoanalysis is also freedom. For Freud this comes about through a remembrance of the past and an understanding of its meaning. Since psycho-analysis is limited to the mental, the mind, through psycho-analysis, can become free only by investigating itself—to "liberate itself to itself." This is as much a Hegelian notion as it is a Freudian one. Hegel writes about

[60] Ibid., 184.

those parts of the mind which need to be liberated, those parts of the mind which are not really one's own:

> To begin with, I do not as yet have full command over the images slumbering in the mine or pit of my inwardness, am not as yet able to recall them at will. No one knows what an infinite host of images of the past slumbers in him; now and then they do indeed accidentally awake, but one cannot, as it is said, call them to mind. Thus the images are *ours* only in a *formal* manner.[61]

This "mine or pit" is what Freud would later call the unconscious.

After the passage just quoted, Hegel goes on to talk about recollection, how the images of the past can become ours. When one considers Freud's description of the transference phenomenon as "a reflection of the past," the process of analysis sounds much like Hegel's "Remembrance": "The manner in which the images of the past lying hidden in the dark depths of our inner being become our actual possession, is that they present themselves to our intelligence in the luminous, plastic shape of an *existent* intuition of *similar* content, and with the help of this *present* intuition we recognize them as intuitions we have already had."[62] The point here is that both Hegel and Freud have a similar view of recollection, and that both view the process as essential for the mind coming to know itself. Both recognize freedom as the result of this process.

Hegel's description of something like the unconscious and of the process of recollection in *The Philosophy of Mind* is deepened by certain lines of thought in *The Philosophy of History*. In the introduction to this set of lectures there is a passage whose meaning is strikingly similar to essential facets of psycho-analysis: "The History of the World begins with its general aim—the realization of the Idea of Spirit—only in an implicit form (*an sich*), that is, as Nature; a hidden, most

---

[61] Ibid., 205.
[62] Ibid.

profoundly hidden, unconscious instinct; and the whole process of History (as already observed), is directed to rendering this unconscious impulse a conscious one.[63]

Freud's concern with the history of the person is also a concern with rendering the unconscious impulse into a conscious one. The substance of his thought is close to Hegel's here: by finding the meaning in the past, psycho-analysis makes the past that is "slumbering in the mine or pit" of the analysand part of the "progress of the consciousness of freedom."[64] Without this consciousness (which Hegel calls self-consciousness) freedom is only an empty, formal concept, accidental and contingent. For both Hegel and Freud, acknowledging meaning in the past is essential for fully being in the present. This is, as I showed with Freud's work, because the past remains intimately bound up with the present through the unconscious. The dialectical relationship between the infantile stages emphasized above made this connection clear. Similarly, Hegel's "Spirit" does not transcend the past, but like the mind, according to Freud, negates and preserves it:

> We have, in traversing the past—however extensive its periods—only to do with what is present: . . . The life of the ever present Spirit is a circle of progressive embodiments, which looked at in one aspect still exist beside each other, and only looked at from another point of view appear as past. The grades which Spirit seems to have left behind it, it still possesses in the depths of its present.[65]

The past is contained in the density of the present, in the layers of the mind. To know that past, to *grasp* it, is to *be* in the present. This is the Hegelian and Freudian conception of freedom.

Hegel's concepts of necessity and reconciliation compli-

---

[63] *The Philosophy of History*, trans. J. Sibree (New York, 1956), 25.

[64] Hegel defines history as the "progress in the consciousness of Freedom," in *The Philosophy of History*, 19.

[65] *The Philosophy of History*, 79.

cate his notion of freedom considerably, however. An explication of the relationship between these three concepts[66] may further illuminate facets of Freud's idea of freedom. In the *Logic*, the first part of *The Encyclopaedia of the Philosophical Sciences*, freedom is described as "the truth of necessity."[67] Hegel rejects the common idea of simple freedom of choice because this freedom is immediate and contingent. That is, the choosing situation is not a result of the person's will, and the situation determines the options and hence the limits of the "free choice." Hegel must be quoted at length here:

> When more narrowly examined, free choice is seen to be in contradiction, to this extent that its form and content stand in antithesis. The matter of choice is given, and known as a content dependent not on the will itself, but on outward circumstances. In reference to such a given content, freedom lies only in the form of choosing, which as it is only a freedom in form, may consequently be regarded as freedom only in supposition. On an ultimate analysis it will be seen that the same outwardness of circumstances, on which is founded the content that the will finds to its hand, can alone account for the will giving its decision for the one and not the other of the two alternatives.[68]

The contingency of the options with which the person is confronted destroys the notion that the will is free in the immediate choosing situation—free in the sense that the will could have chosen any of the options found available. The person must come to understand the history of the situation itself—why this apparent contingency is in fact a *necessity*, given what had come before it. Indeed, the truly necessary event, Hegel claims, has within it its own antecedents; it is "simple self-relation."[69] At the start of the interpretation of

---

[66] The words "concept," "notion," and "ideas" are not used here in the technical sense which Hegel established for them.

[67] *Logic: Being Part One of the Encyclopaedia of the Philosophical Sciences*, trans. W. Wallace (Oxford, 1975), 220.

[68] Ibid., 206.

[69] Ibid., 208.

the situation, circumstances seem truly to be contingent; they are "just there." Reflection, however, finds a meaning in these apparently arbitrary circumstances, the necessity for their present existence: "The process of necessity begins with the existence of scattered circumstances which appear to have no interconnection and no concern with one another." But, Hegel continues: "Necessity is blind only so long as it is not understood."[70]

I take Hegel's project here to be the same as Freud's was seen to be in *The Interpretation of Dreams* when he makes the claim that all ideas are "purposive"—one must grasp the reasons they are as they are; in giving them meaning and direction, one sees their necessity. The passage concerning purposive ideas, quoted in part above, can now be more fully understood:

> For it is demonstrably untrue that we are being carried along a purposeless stream of ideas when, in the process of inter-preting a dream, we abandon reflection and allow involuntary ideas to emerge. It can be shown that all that we can ever get rid of are purposive ideas that are *known* to us; as soon as we have done this, *unknown*—or, as we inaccurately say, "uncon-scious"—purposive ideas take charge and thereafter determine the course of the involuntary ideas. No influence that we can bring to bear upon our mental processes can ever enable us to think without purposive ideas; nor am I aware of any states of psychical confusion which can do so.[71]

The freedom found at the close of the transference is a free-dom that is based on re-collecting and acknowledging one's personal history—recognizing the necessity, the "purpose," in the chaotic past. Necessity is intimately bound up with meaning for both Hegel and Freud. The link between neces-sity and meaning leads Freud to claim that "only a man who had had Leonardo's childhood experiences could have painted

---

[70] Ibid., 208–209. Notice here the same juxtaposition of interpretation and determinism found in Freud.

[71] *The Interpretation of Dreams*, SE, v, 528.

the Mona Lisa and the St. Anne,"[72] and Hegel to claim that necessity is not blind but seeing.[73]

There is an aspect of Hegel's conception of freedom that is incompatible with Freud's account but that nevertheless illuminates the psycho-analytic notion of freedom. This is the idea of "reconciliation" found in *The Phenomenology of Spirit*.[74] The most important discussion of reconciliation is found in the last section of "Spirit," part BB of the work. It is here that the struggle between two individuals, two "I's" as Hegel phrases it, is ended through a mutual forgiveness and a realization of the universal duality of the self and the other.[75] In this moment of unity with the universal, "Absolute Spirit"— the unity of the subjective and objective in knowledge—makes its "implicit appearance" in the world: the sufferings of the past are reconciled in their final end; redemption is at hand. The final end is Wisdom, and its appearance in an individual, Hegel. The final synthesis of the dialectic is in the wise man; the mind and mind are united in knowledge. The progress of the consciousness of freedom is complete; history, then, is over.[76]

Freud's concept of freedom does not contain any notion of forgiveness or a redemption of the past. It is here that Freud and Hegel part company. Freud, like Hegel, showed that self-consciousness comes as a result of struggle: as a result of domination and profound alienation. Hegel's ultimate forgiveness, spirit at home with itself, does not enter

[72] *Leonardo*, SE, XI, 136.

[73] *Logic*, 209.

[74] "Reconciliation" is almost identical with the *Logic*'s "Consolation," 209–211.

[75] *Phenomenology of Spirit*, trans. A. V. Miller (Oxford, 1977), 409.

[76] For a detailed account of the completion of history in Hegel, see Alexandre Kojève, *Introduction to the Reading of Hegel*, trans. J. Nichols, Jr. (New York, 1969), especially 75–100. For an explication of some of the major issues of the idea of the "end of history" see: Michael S. Roth, "A Problem of Recognition: Alexandre Kojève and the End of History," *History and Theory*, 24 (1985), 293–306; Barry Cooper, *The End of History: An Essay on Modern Hegelianism* (Toronto, 1984); Michael S. Roth, "Knowing and History: The Resurgence of French Hegelianism from the 1930's through the Post-War Period," Ph.D. diss., Princeton University, 1983.

into the psycho-analytic situation. Hegel describes the final synthesis as follows: "The reconciling *Yea*, in which the two 'I's' let go their antithetical *existence*, is the *existence* of the 'I' which has expanded into a duality, and therein remains identical with itself, and, in its complete externalization and opposite, possesses the certainty of itself: it is God manifested in the midst of those who know themselves in the form of pure knowledge."[77] This "reconciling affirmation" is possibly only because of Hegel's belief that "the wounds of the Spirit heal, and leave no scars behind."[78] This indicates the full redemption of the past in the Absolute. Freud denies that the struggle of spirit with itself leaves no scars. Indeed, the task of psycho-analysis is precisely to examine the scars of the spirit—and not to remove them, but to apprehend their meaning. Conflicts are laid bare by psycho-analysis, not resolved. Psycho-analysis enables the subject to reach the point where he can make his choices with a knowledge of the meaning, of the necessity, of the options with which he is confronted. In Freud's conception of the mind, the dialectic remains unresolved; knowing is not resolution. As Lacan says: "The radical heteronomy that Freud's discovery shows gaping within man can never again be covered over without whatever is used to hide it being profoundly dishonest."[79] The freedom of the analysand at the end of the transference is the knowing of this "radical heteronomy," the opportunity to act self-consciously on the basis of this knowing.

Thus, the acknowledging and freedom that emerge out of the transference confront the individual with the connection between his own personal history and the demands of his civilization. We shall examine in detail in the next chapter some of the implications that psycho-analysis has for understanding this connection. The dialectical contradictions of desire are apprehended through a historical interpretation. The contradictions are, for Freud as for Hegel, the impetus behind both thought and action. The transference, manifest-

[77] *Phenomenology*, 409.
[78] Ibid., 407.
[79] *Ecrits: A Selection*, 172.

ing these contradictions, leads not necessarily to any specific activity, but to the creation of a *radical sensibility*—a sensibility that understands *the roots* of the contradictions with which it is faced. The transference reveals the costs of action; the sacrifice in the *effort* to change a way of life significantly. There is no forgiveness here, no transcendence to a stage of being in which all the earlier stages somehow vanish from the depths of the mind. Aggression and sexuality will still have to be dealt with after such changes, if we take Freud seriously. A post-transference consciousness in modern society would realize the depths of ambivalence as well as the depths of contradictions between the desires of men and women and the realities of civilization. A change in history, and not merely a repetition in the service of the death instinct, may become possible when the consciousness of the dynamics of change itself has been created. When this self-consciousness is achieved, the psychological precondition for constructive radical action is created.

Transference, then, is the radical facet of Freud's theory because it reveals the contradictions—and contradictions are not merely abstract oppositions, but mean real pain for persons—that can lead people to make fundamental changes in the way they live together. Although it does not compel such changes, transference makes possible an understanding of some of the roots of the crisis of our civilization. Negation through acknowledgment and action is not an escape from the past, but like all negations, a form of preservation as well. This hard fact of dialectical awareness must be an essential part of any self-conscious effort at change. The transference is a vehicle for such an awareness; it presents the meaning made through the theory of history to the person so that he or she can know the pain of a past unconsciously bound up in the present. Perhaps when the depths of this pain can be grasped and not merely suffered, acknowledgment, negation, and freedom can begin to be realized.

THE ANALOGY
WITH THE GROUP

5

Psycho-Analysis
and the Group

Since my mental powers have revived, I have been
working in a field where you will be surprised to meet
me. I have unearthed strange and uncanny things.

Freud to Jung, August 20, 1911

Until now, this book has been almost exclusively
concerned with what I have been calling the most crucial
theoretical developments in Freud's work: concerned, that is,
with the psycho-analytic investigation of the individual. This
emphasis has probably evoked curiosity in the reader. One
expects a work concerned with psycho-analysis as a theory
of history to deal with the psycho-analytic speculations on
culture and the origins of civilization. But any interpretation
of Freud's writings that does not examine in detail his investigations of the dynamics of individual thought and action is
an interpretation built on sand. To say the same thing differ-
ently: Freud's work becomes relevant to history, and to political action, only because of his theories of the individual. Although Freud's speculations on the dynamics of the group
are important for an understanding of his corpus, they must
be seen in relation to their foundation in the theory of the
individual. This chapter examines Freud's development of the
analogy between the individual and the group. The emphasis
here will be on the most systematic exposition of that anal-

ogy, *Group Psychology and the Analysis of the Ego* (1921).[1] A full explication of this book will not be attempted, but I will investigate some of the ways in which the theory of dreams, the theory of repression, and the theory of infantile sexuality have played and can play roles in the application of psychoanalysis to the group. Finally, the importance of the concepts of sublimation and the transference will be examined in relation to the group.

In the first section of this work my explication of the three most important elements of Freud's theories led to the conclusion that psycho-analysis is first and foremost a theory of history aimed at the establishment of a more complete consciousness in the person than had previously existed. In the second section the theory of the transference was shown to reveal the connection between history and negation in Freud's work. The final object of psycho-analysis is the resolution of the transference in the freedom to choose, think, and act; the final object, we might say, is the creation of radical sensibility, a sensibility that has acknowledged the roots of its conflicts. In this third section I try to show that this radical sensibility—this "post-transference consciousness"—is not destroyed or made less meaningful at the group level. On the contrary, I try to show that the psycho-analytic response to the problems that arise in relation to the freedom that can result from the transference deepens the notion of participation in groups and the possibility for creating significant, self-conscious thought and action at the group level.

I

As dreams are the royal road to the unconscious for psycho-analysis, the structure of the approach to dreams was

[1] Other texts will be examined in this chapter. Aspects of *Totem and Taboo* (to which the letter quoted in the epigraph refers) and *Civilization and Its Discontents* will be looked at in some detail, but the focus will remain on *Group Psychology and the Analysis of the Ego*, SE, xviii, and references to page of this work will appear in the text.

our paradigm for all psycho-analytic investigations of the individual mind. Groups, however, do not dream, at least not in the same way as persons do. It is certainly difficult to conceive of sleep as the activity of a group, and the relaxation of the censorship in the state of sleep is essential for the appearance of repressed material in dreams. Also, the wish to sleep plays an important role in allowing this material to appear. The question of group dreaming not only involves the problem of an analogy to the state of sleep at the group level; it also requires some investigation of the existence of the following: a group unconscious (and therefore of some kind of group mind); repression and some type of dreamwork at the group level; desires and wishes of the group; and the function and meaning of an interpretation with regard to the "group dream." These problems will be addressed throughout this chapter.

The question of dream theory in relation to the group immediately opens up many of the problems of group psychology generally. It is appropriate, then, to examine Freud's preliminary remarks on the relation between individual and group psychology. On the first page of *Group Psychology and the Analysis of the Ego* he points to the social character of individual psychology: "In the individual's mental life someone else is invariably involved, as a model, as an object, as a helper, as an opponent; and so from the very first individual psychology, in this extended but entirely justifiable sense of the words, is at the same time social psychology as well" (69). The chief areas of psycho-analytic research almost always involve more than just the single person. These areas—such as the oedipal situation and the transference relationship—can, however, be distinguished from group psychology in a more narrow sense. As Freud notes:

Now in speaking of social or group psychology it has become usual to leave these relations (where the individual is under the influence of a single or small number of persons) on one side and to isolate as the subject of inquiry the influencing of an individual by a large number of people simultaneously. . . .

> Group psychology is therefore concerned with the individual
> man as a member of a race, of a nation, of a caste, of a profes-
> sion, of an institution, or as a component part of a crowd of
> people who have been organized into a group at some partic-
> ular time and for some definite purpose. [70]

This passage effectively defines the object of the psycho-analytic study of the group.

Freud is deeply concerned with the question of "group
mind." The second section of *Group Psychology* is entitled
"Le Bon's Description of the Group Mind."[2] Gustave Le Bon,
Freud tells the reader, thinks that the coming together of individuals in a group puts the members in possession of a
collective mind "which makes them feel, think, and act in a
manner quite different from that in which each individual of
them would feel, think and act were he in a state of isola-
tion"(73). The three reasons Le Bon gives for this change of
character are the loss of responsibility through anonymity,
contagion, and suggestibility.

Freud, as one might expect, does not give much credence
to the idea that participation in the group involves the appearance of new characteristics. His claim is that participation in the group results in the release of hidden desires that
are present in the individual as well. "Group mind," then, is
the collection of these common hidden drives.

> As we should say, the mental superstructure, the development
> of which in individuals shows such dissimilarities, is removed,
> and the unconscious foundations, which are similar in every-
> one, stand exposed to view. . . . From our point of view we
> need not attribute so much importance to the appearance of
> new characteristics. For us it would be enough to say that in a

---

[2] Freud concentrates on Le Bon's 1895 work *Psychologie des foules*. This
was translated as *The Crowd: A Study of the Popular Mind* (New York, 1896).
I am not concerned with a close reading of Le Bon's book, but only with
the role it plays in *Group Psychology*. For a detailed consideration of Freud's
use of Le Bon, see Philip Rieff, "The Origins of Freud's Political Psychology,"
Journal of the History of Ideas, 17 (1956), 235–249.

group the individual is brought under conditions which allow him to throw off the repressions of his unconscious instinctual impulses. [74]

The release of unconscious mental forces in the group calls to mind the release provided by dreams. In both instances the primitive desires of the unconscious are able to find expression when inhibitions are relaxed. Freud points out this analogy with the dream process, which is perhaps seen most clearly in the group's ability to hold contradictory ideas without conflict (79). The predominance of illusion and the tendency for the group to emphasize emotions and wishes are paralleled in dreams by the lack of intellectual coherence and the basis in wish fulfillment. As Freud says: "Indeed, just as in dreams and hypnosis, in the mental operations of a group the function for testing the reality of things falls into the background in comparison with the strength of wishful impulses with their affective cathexis" (80). To find an analogy to dreaming at the group level, it is surely not sufficient to point out how some of the elements of the individual's participation in the group correspond to elements of the dream process. The preeminence of unconscious factors in the operations of the group may be crucial, but the analogue to the dream itself is still a mystery. In other words, dreams are the royal road to the unconscious because they reveal the desires of the person—as well as the distortions to which these desires are subject—through the course of interpretation. In the description of group mind presented so far, it is unclear what the object of interpretation would be at the group level. If the group is led primarily by the unconscious, what product of the group serves as the path to meaning on which psycho-analysis can travel?

Freud avoids this question at the beginning of *Group Psychology* by focusing on Le Bon's description of the group rather than on any particular group itself. Some of his remarks in the postscript to this work, though, make clear that Freud regarded the myth as the analogue to the dream at the group level. The myth that the analyst is able to read or

141

hear is analogous to the dream report. The analyst can come to see the wish behind the myth through interpretation, the distortions that conceal the wish, and the functions that the myth serves for the group. Freud follows just this pattern in his comments on fairy tales (136). He sees the animals who help the hero as representations of the brothers in the primal horde, and the hero's task as a displacement of the primal crime into a more acceptable domain. The myth, although at one time the product of an individual author, is valuable to the interpreter because the group has accepted it. The tale represented the members' unconscious longings, and it allowed them to identify with the hero. Through interpretation, the meaning of these desires can be made clearer. "The poet," Freud tells the reader, "disguised the truth with lies in accordance with his longing" (136). These lies are given form—the epic or the fairy tale—and presented to the group. The poet, Freud explains, "goes and relates to the group his hero's deeds which he invented. At bottom this hero is no one but himself. Thus he lowers himself to the level of reality, and raises his hearers to the level of imagination. But his hearers understand the poet, and, in virtue of their having the same relation of longing towards the primal father, they can identify themselves with the hero" (136–137).

Freud recognized the myth as a dreamlike structure as early as *The Interpretation of Dreams*. The appearance of symbols of a universal character in dreams led him to turn to myths in his exploration of typical dreams. Freud was struck by the occurrence of dreams that did not seem to be the product of any individual experiences, and noted that "in complete contrast" to the individual nature of dreaming, "there are a certain number of dreams which almost everyone has dreamt alike and which we are accustomed to assume must have the same meaning for everyone."[3] These dreams seem to stem from a portion of the unconscious which is not a product of a person's particular experience and which is somehow common to all persons.

[3] *The Interpretation of Dreams*, SE, IV, 241.

It was pointed out in Chapter 1 above that representation by symbols in dreams seemed to jeopardize the psycho-analytic claim that dream interpretation was primarily carried out by the dreamer. In the theory of the individual, the technique of dream interpretation by means of symbols was made subordinate to interpretation through free association. On the group level there is no dreamer who will provide associations. At any rate, since the myth makes use of symbols rather than individual experience, any associations with these symbols would only tend to obscure them. As Freud writes in *The Interpretation of Dreams*: "If we attempt to interpret a typical dream, the dreamer fails as a rule to produce the associations which would in other cases have led us to understand it, or else his associations become obscure and insufficient so that we cannot solve our problem with their help."[4] Associations are helpful in the interpretation of a typical dream only to arrive at the dream's meaning for the dreamer, and not for the translation of any particular dream element. That is, the associations enable the analysand to understand why he made use of the symbol in his dream at the time he did so. The associations can lead to the uncovering of the particular wish behind the typical dream.

In the myth of the hero that Freud comments on in *Group Psychology*, the dreamer's associations are replaced by the reports of the way the myth is treated by the group. Although Freud speculates on the motivations of the author of the mythic poem, the essential element is the group's acceptance of it. This acceptance is indeed what elevates the poem or the tale to the status of myth. In the myth of the hero, the story of the heroic deed becomes a vehicle for an identification with the hero and his eventual deification. The analyst is confronted with the "symptom" of this process, the group as followers of a deity, and the text of the "dream," the poet's construction. This construction conceals a meaning that has been distorted and "revised" over time. Other myths, legends, and folk tales supply additional material for the ana-

[4] Ibid.

lyst's construction of a historical interpretation of the connections among these elements. The analyst is not left only
with a series of symbols which he is forced to translate according to a fixed key. Although he has no free associations
with which to work, he does have the signs of the way the
tale was accepted, and, eventually, as a vehicle for wish fulfillment, turned into a myth.

The missing component in the analogy between the dream
and the myth is the analysand. Although the analyst can make
use of the signs of the way the tale was accepted and eventually turned into a myth, he is not in dialogue with an
analysand who will respond to his reconstructions of these
signs. In individual analysis, the response to the analyst's
interpretation is an essential component of the search for
meaning.[5] In the interpretation of myths, the analyst must
depend upon the function that the myth has served for its
hearers and readers in the present as well as the past. Freud
makes use of this approach in his examination of the Oedipus legend in *The Interpretation of Dreams*. He does not claim
that the Greeks had a special psychic constitution that led
them to regard the drama in a certain way, but rather, he points
to the legend's effect on its audience through its use of material that is an essential part of the development of persons:

> His [Oedipus'] destiny moves us only because it might have
> been ours—because the oracle laid the same curse upon us
> before our birth as upon him. It is the fate of all of us, perhaps,
> to direct our first sexual impulse towards our mother and our
> first hatred and our first murderous wish against our father.
> Our dreams convince us that it is so. . . . While the poet, as
> he unravels the past, brings to light the guilt of Oedipus, he is
> at the same time compelling us to recognize our own inner
> minds, in which those same impulses, though suppressed, are
> still to be found.[6]

[5] See Freud, "Constructions in Analysis" (1937), *SE*, xxiii, 255–269.
[6] *The Interpretation of Dreams*, *SE*, iv, 262–263.

144

This method of interpretation—finding the meaning of the myth through its meaning for us—is characteristic of psycho-analytic interpretation generally.

Freud seems to be aware of the problematic value of interpretation without a process that includes associations. He credits the interpretation if it "brings coherence and understanding into more and more new regions" (122). He also refers to the hypothesis of the primal horde in *Totem and Taboo* as "a scientific myth" (135). The analyst's construction has no privileged place; it is an attempt to bring meaning to the signs with which we are confronted.[7]

The question with which the discussion of the group dream began—what is the analogue to the state of sleep at the group level?—can now be answered. The relaxation of the censorship occurs when the poet "raises his hearers to the level of the imagination" (135). Because of the *form* of the tale the hearers are able to participate in the release it can bring. Their longing for the father can be satisfied by the myth's distortions and by their own identification with the hero. The threatening nature of this longing is diffused because it is expressed in *merely a tale*. The stories we tell ourselves enable us to make connections which we desire but which, outside the form of a common story, we deny ourselves. As we are "raised to the level of the imagination" we attain some satisfaction; and as a group we evade the censorship.[8]

---

[7] Freud compares interpretation and delusion at the close of his investigation of the paranoid, Dr. Schreber. See Freud, *Psycho-Analytic Notes of an Autobiographical Account of a Case of Paranoia (Dementia Paranoides)* (1911), *SE*, XII, 79; and "Constructions in Analysis," *SE*, XXIII, 265–269.

[8] One of the major influences on Freud's speculations on mythology in *Group Psychology* was the work of Otto Rank. Rank first explored the relationship between dreams and myths in *Der Künstler*, published in 1907, and continued to do so in his later work. See, for example, *The Myth of the Birth of the Hero and Other Writings*, ed. P. Freund (New York, 1964). Karl Abraham's *Dreams and Myths: A Study in Race Psychology*, trans. W. White, Nervous and Mental Disease Monograph, 15 (New York, 1913), shows elements of the dreamwork in the myth, but it is mostly of historical interest. The literature on myth interpretation and psycho-analysis—as well as Jungian psychology—is extensive and listed in many works.

The reader should note that dream interpretation plays an important

145

II

As in the theory of the individual, the concept of repression clarifies and helps complete the dream theory in the investigation of the group. In the discussion of myth as the analogue to the dream at the group level, the unconscious elements of group formation were pointed out. As Freud notes, following Le Bon, there is a relaxation of inhibitions in the group as well as the appearance of desires that would otherwise have remained unconscious. Freud's description hardly sounds like something to which repression would be relevant: "Nothing about it [the group] is premeditated. Though it may desire things passionately, yet this is never so for long, for it is incapable of perseverance. It cannot tolerate any delay between its desire and the fulfillment of what it desires. It has a sense of omnipotence; the notion of impossibility disappears for the individual in the group" (77). Yet in spite of this apparently uninhibited character, one is quickly led by "firmly established linguistic usage"[9]—that is, by the phrase "political repression," the meaning of which is independent of any psycho-analytic connotations—to consider seriously the possibility of an analogue to repression at the group level. "Political repression" here refers to the way in which a government—in a broad sense—or a regime inhibits the practi-

---

role in some modern forms of psychoanalytically informed group psychotherapy. Often the group itself acts as the interpreter of the dream. See, for example: Alexander Wolf, "The Psychoanalysis of Groups," in *Group Psychotherapy and Group Function*, ed. M. Rosenbaum and M. Berger (New York, 1963), 233–288; Morris Brody and Saul Harrison, "Stutterers," in *The Fields of Group Psychotheraphy*, ed. S. R. Slavson (New York, 1956), 102–103; Alexander Wolf and Emanuel K. Scwartz, *Psychoanalysis in Groups* (New York, 1962), 135–161; Irvin D. Yalom, *The Theory and Practice of Group Psychotherapy*, 2d ed. (New York, 1975), 432–436; Helen E. Durkin, *The Group in Depth* (New York, 1964), 259–260. Siegmund Foulkes also emphasized the "group dream" as material for group interpretation, but emphasized that, in contrast to individual analysis, attention to the manifest content's connection to "here-and-now" concerns was important in group psychoanalysis. See, for example, S. H. Foulkes and E. J. Anthony, *Group Psychotherapy: The Psychoanalytic Approach* (Baltimore, 1965), 131, 151, 173; and S. H. Foulkes, *Therapeutic Group Analysis* (New York, 1965), 126–128, 165–166.

[9]See above, p. 47.

146

cal social activity of some, or all, members of a group. In *Group Psychology*, Freud examines this process through the concept of identification.

One may safely say that in *Group Psychology* identification is the central psycho-analytic concept for understanding the formation and maintenance of groups. Identification plays the central role in the relationship between the leader of the group and the followers, and this is where the concept immediately seems to be relevant to political repression, but it is also significant in Freud's interpretation of the relationship among the followers.

Freud begins the chapter on identification with some general remarks on the psycho-analytic use of the concept. "Identification," he says, "is known to psycho-analysis as the earliest expression of an emotional tie with another person" (105). He goes on to make the distinction between identification with the father and the choice of the father as an object: "In the first case one's father is what one would like to *be*, and in the second he is what one would like to *have*. The distinction, that is, depends upon whether the tie attaches to the subject or to the object of the ego. The former kind of tie is therefore already possible before any sexual object-choice has been made" (106). Identification, then, is located at the beginning of the child's attempts at object relations. It is characteristic of the earliest stage of life and can be returned to in later years through regression. This return, Freud says, is often a product of a situation marked by repression: "it often happens that under the conditions in which symptoms are constructed, that is, where there is repression and where mechanisms of the unconscious are dominant, object-choice is turned back into identification—the ego assumes the characteristics of the object" (107).

Freud goes on to describe another type of identification in which a person perceives a quality that he shares in common with an object and identifies himself with that object or with the common quality. In this way a person may acquire a hysteric's symptom through an identification with the hysteric or with the symptom itself.

147

There are, then, three types of identification enumerated in *Group Psychology*: (1) the original form of the emotional relation to an object; (2) the regression in a situation marked by repression from an object-choice to an identification; (3) the process of identification on the basis of a common trait. The first, of course, is the basis for the two that follow.

In the group, Freud says, these processes make up the crux of the relationships between the leader and the rest of the group, and among the members themselves. The members take the leader as the ideal representation of themselves— take him, that is, in place of their ego ideal.[10] The leader represents the idealized father who the child wanted to be and could never become. The leader—or, more accurately, the person's perception of the leader—assumes the place of the ego ideal and takes over the functions of this agency. These functions are: "self-observation, the moral conscience, the censorship of dreams, and the chief influence in repression" (110). This last function is of utmost importance here. As the member identifies with the leader—as he takes the leader as his ego ideal—the member becomes part of a new psychical system in a complex way. That is, the powers of repression and censorship previously held by facets of the member's personality which took his desires and their conflicts as the basis for repression are now held by the representation of a figure that is a stranger to the history of the person's desires. This process is extraordinary. Not only does this identification mean that the individual has lost a portion of the ability

[10]The ego ideal is an agency that results from narcissism and the identification with the parents. The term first appears in "On Narcissism: An Introduction" (*SE*, xiv) in 1914. The "ego ideal" is certainly the conceptual forerunner of the "superego," and the two terms are used synonymously in *The Ego and the Id* (1923). Some analysts, however, prefer to keep the two terms distinct, the ego ideal as loving and the superego as punitive. Christopher Lasch uses this distinction in his discussion of narcissism and the possibilities for transcending it in *The Minimal Self: Psychic Survivial in Troubled Times* (New York, 1984), 173–185. He also presents a handy bibliography of the relevant literature, pp. 284–286. I will not in this essay attempt to find a psychic agency on which to pin our hopes, or even on which to found them. Hence, I shall follow Freud in not distinguishing the ego ideal from the superego.

to determine the way he will act given his desires and ambivalences—after all, one expects precisely that in group formation—but also, the very power to dream and seek satisfaction has been shifted from the individual to the leader of the
group. "Political repression," in this psycho-analytic sense,
runs so deep as to be part of the way we figure our identity;
there is no turning away from the authority of repression.

A few qualifying remarks are necessary here. It is not clear
how meaningful it is to speak of the ego ideal as being part
of the individual prior to any identification with the leader.
After all, the ideal itself is the product of a series of identifications and never something that the individual consciously
controls. The ego ideal is modeled on the father through an
identification that takes place in early childhood. Freud's
analysis of the leader-follower relationship is so striking,
though, because it points to an *ongoing psychological need
in persons to reconstitute the ideal through relationships of
dependency*. The child's fears and eventual subordination in
the oedipal situation are repeated at the level of the group.
It seems that the process of identification that results in a
reconstitution of the ego ideal is basic to the individual's activity in the social context. Repression in this context—and
repression of the individual's desires is still meant here—
becomes the function of the perceived leader. As the ego ideal,
the leader can instill a sense of joy in the followers or a tre-
mendous sense of guilt. "There is always a feeling of triumph
when something in the ego coincides with the ego ideal,"
Freud notes. "And the sense of guilt (as well as the sense of
inferiority) can also be understood as an expression of tension between the ego and the ego ideal" (131).

The way in which the members of the group take the leader
as their ego ideal is related to the third type of identification
discussed above, identification on the basis of a common trait.
The members of the group identify with each other on the
basis of their respective identifications with the leader. This
is perhaps most readily seen in the context of Freud's discussion of two artificial groups (groups in which "a certain
external force is employed to keep them from disintegrating"

149

[93]), the church and the army. In the former Christ is the leader whom the adherents identify as their ideal. They are bound together by this identification and by the idea that the leader loves all his followers equally. All the followers stand in the same relation to the ideal. All are as egos to the ego ideal; any feelings of rivalry are checked by the ideal's prohibitions as well as by the difficulty of giving up the security of sharing in the same dependent relationship with others. This phenomenon leads Freud to say, "There is no doubt that the tie which unites each individual with Christ is also the cause of the tie which unites them with one another" (94). These ties are the ties of identification. The binding of the members together in their dependency on the leader has ominous consequences when seen in the context of repression.

This discussion of repression in terms of identification has left untouched the fundamental question of how repression can be applied to the group. In the theory of the individual, repression consists in the pushing of the prohibited drive or threatening idea into the unconscious. There the idea or drive "proliferates in the dark" and emerges in some other form. At the group level, the following question arises: If there is repression in groups, where does the impulse or idea get repressed to? Another problem that needs examination is the distinction between group repression and the repression of the individual in a group. The leader's role vis-à-vis the followers through identification is certainly an example of repression at the group level, but it seems to be the repression of the desires of individuals in the group and not the desires of the group itself.

Freud's remarks on the inhibition of sexual aims in the group help clarify this distinction between individual and group desire, as well as the problem of whether one can meaningfully speak of a "group unconscious." Recall the beginning of this chapter in which Freud's discussion of Le Bon's notion of group mind was examined. "Unconscious" is used by Le Bon in the discussion of group mind in the descriptive sense, and not to mean the repressed, or a topographical division of the mind (75).[11] Le Bon speaks of the "genius of the race": the unconscious substratum of common characteristics that are brought into the open in group activity. Freud rephrases Le Bon's description: "As we should say, the mental superstructure, the development of which in individuals shows such dissimilarities, is removed, and the unconscious foundations, which are similar in everyone, stand exposed to view" (74). Sexual urges are, of course, part of these unconscious foundations that are common to everyone. These urges, however, must be inhibited in the group. That is, although the group relies on the sexual ties of identification just discussed, genital sexuality must be repressed. The genital aim, Freud says, physiologically requires two persons; a third is superfluous. He notes: "Two people coming together for the purpose of sexual satisfaction, in so far as they seek for solitude, are making a demonstration against the herd instinct, the group feeling. The more they are in love the more completely they suffice for each other" (140).

Group ties depend, then, on an inhibition of what might be called "pairing." Pairing separates two persons from the group, and hence from the intense, and equal, identification with its other members.[12] Also, the sexual attachment threatens the place of the leader of the group; his role as the ego ideal is put in jeopardy. In this instance of repression at the group level, then, desires that are common to the members are inhibited. The question still remains, however, where these desires are repressed to. If it is meaningful to speak of a group unconscious in this regard, then group symptoms and group neuroses become important areas for psycho-analytic inquiry.

Another example of the inhibition of the sexual drive at the group level sheds light on the question of a group unconscious. In *Totem and Taboo* Freud put forward his "primal

[11] See Le Bon, *The Crowd: A Study of the Popular Mind* (New York, 1896), 26–38.
[12] On "pairing" see W. R. Bion's remarks in, *Experiences in Groups and Other Papers* (New York, 1959), 61–63; also Wolf and Schwartz, *Psychoanalysis in Groups*, 107–108; Durkin, *The Group in Depth*, 45–54.

horde hypothesis." He described the origins of religion and civilization by speculating that a band of brothers killed their tyrannical father and tried to manage the guilt that ensued from the killing. The sons renounce their desires for the women of the group—which had been the motive for killing the father—to preserve the group. Their bond of identification was too great to allow deadly rivalry to arise over the women. This bond was strengthened by their sense of guilt from the killing. In *Totem and Taboo*, to which Freud refers at the end of *Group Psychology*, he is clear about the necessity for the brothers to repress their sexual desires if the group is to continue to exist:

> Sexual desires do not unite men but divide them. Though the brothers had banded together in order to overcome their father, they were all one another's rivals in regard to the women. Each of them would have wished, like his father, to have all the women to himself. The new organization would have collapsed in a struggle of all against all, for none of them was of such overmastering strength as to be able to take on his father's part with success. Thus the brothers had no alternative, if they were to live together, but—not, perhaps, until they had passed through many dangerous crises—to institute the law against incest, by which they all renounced the women whom they desired and who had been their chief motive for despatching their father. In this way they rescued the organization which had made them strong.[13]

In this story of the primal horde one sees the first, and most important, example of repression at the group level. Desires that the brothers held in common are denied; the law against incest is created and the group defined by exogamy. If Freud is making use of the concept of a group unconscious in his work, its origin should be in this renunciation by the band of brothers.

Two years after the publication of *Totem and Taboo*, in a

---

[13] *Totem and Taboo* (1913), *SE*, XIII, 144; on the "primal horde hypothesis," see 140–146.

1915 essay entitled "The Unconscious," Freud points to the inherited mental formations that he thinks are contained in the mind. "The content of the *Ucs.* [Unconscious] may be compared with an aboriginal population in the mind," he writes. "If inherited formations exist in the human being— something analogous to instinct *(Instinkt)* in animals—these constitute the nucleus of the *Ucs.* Later there is added to them what is discarded during childhood development as unserviceable; and this need not differ in its nature from what is inherited."[14] Later, in *Group Psychology*, he continues this train of thought:

> Le Bon's unconscious more especially contains the most deeply buried features of the racial mind, which as a matter of fact lies outside the scope of psycho-analysis. We do not fail to recognize, indeed, that the ego's nucleus, which comprises the "archaic heritage" of the human mind, is unconscious; but in addition to this we distinguish the "unconscious repressed," which arose from a portion of that heritage. [75n]

Although he recognizes these aboriginal contents of the mind, Freud clearly emphasizes their appearance in the individual, and the person's reaction to this appearance. In *From the History of an Infantile Neurosis* (1918), he says:

> All that we find in the prehistory of neuroses is that a child catches hold of his phylogenetic experience where his own experience fails him. He fills in the gaps in individual truth with historic truth; he replaces occurrences in his own life by occurrences in the lives of his ancestors. I fully agree with Jung in recognizing the existence of this phylogenetic inheritance; but I regard it as a methodological error to seize upon a phylogenetic explanation before the ontogenetic possibilities have been exhausted.[15]

Freud, then, will talk about the revealing of the common characteristics of a person's unconscious, but seldom of a

---

[14]"The Unconscious," *SE*, xiv, 195. See editor's note on this page.
[15]*From the History of an Infantile Neurosis, SE*, xvii, 97.

special entity like a group, collective, or racial unconscious. His emphasis, even at the level of the group, remains with the particular—or perhaps, the representative—member.[16] Repression at the group level, then, would consist in the desires that the members hold in common being repressed into "their respective unconsciouses." The case of the brothers after the primal crime is illustrative here. The common desire is for the women who had been previously held as property by the father. The repression after the killing consists of each repressing this desire, and each having to manage this repression psychically.

The group becomes crucial in the context of the management of repression. Repression is often the cause of neurosis; the group provides an alternative to neurosis. Freud says neurosis is asocial; it is the individual's attempt to deal with the conflict of his desires. The group offers the individual the opportunity to participate in actions and beliefs that also deal with the conflict of his desires, but that do so in a "socially useful" way.[17] These actions and beliefs may serve to make the group an alternative to neurosis. Freud points out: "It appears that where a powerful impetus has been given to group formation neuroses may diminish, and, at all events temporarily, disappear" (142). The neuroses, he tells the reader, are the individual form of the group's activity: "If he is left to himself, a neurotic is obliged to replace by his own symptom formations the great group formations from which he has been excluded. He creates his own world of imagination for himself, his own religion, his own system of delusions, and thus recapitulates the institutions of humanity in a distorted way" (142). The activities of the group, like the activities of a neurosis, are the products of some form of repression. The individual in the group somehow escapes the pain of neu-

---

[16] See Freud's discussion of collective mind in *Totem and Taboo, SE,* XIII, 157–159.

[17] The question whether some incidence of neuroses is socially useful is not central here. On the social function of the idea of neurosis see, for example, Michel Foucault, *Histoire de la folie a l'âge classique* (Paris, 1961, 1972).

rosis, but the price of this escape is as yet unclear. In the discussion of sublimation below, the mechanism by means of which a group allows its members some satisfaction of their desires and a relaxation of their ambivalences will be examined in detail.

It should now be clear that the concept of repression can be usefully employed at the group level, and that Freud did so in *Group Psychology*. The process of identification proved to be incisive for understanding the psycho-analytic meaning of the phrase "political repression." Freud's examination of the leader-follower relationship deepens the notion of political control. The inhibition of sexual urges in the group seems to indicate that a repression of some kind is always the product of group formation.[18] Freud does not rely on the concept of a collective unconscious, but prefers to speak of the repression of impulses that individual members hold in common.

I examine the concepts of sublimation and the transference below, in part, to consider the meaning of repression at the group level more closely. Since, however, infantile sexual urges are the most important things that a person either represses or sublimates, they must first be considered at the group level.

III

In the discussion of Freud's theory of infantile sexuality above, I focused on three major topics: the historical development of Freud's thought on the subject up to the writing of *Three Essays on the Theory of Sexuality*; the theory of infantile sexual development; and the role of sexuality as the material base of psycho-analysis and as the limit of psycho-analysis to the mental, to the meanings of desire. In this section I will be concerned with the analogous areas at the group level, concentrating on the stages of civilization presented in

[18] See above, Chap. 4, 107–111.

Totem and Taboo. The status Freud gives to his interpretations of the past—especially with regard to historical facts or data—will also be examined.

In the discussion of the analogues of the dream and of repression, we saw that the place of sexuality was already a large one. The myth of the hero centered on the son's wish to overthrow the father in order to have sexual relations with the women. The acceptance of the myth by the members of a group indicates the ease with which they can identify with the hero to deflect their guilt and to satisfy some of their longing for the father Freud says in *Group Psychology* (137). The ties between leader and follower, as well as the ties among the followers themselves are based on certain infantile prototypes. Taking the leader as the ego ideal is a repetition of the relationship between parent and child, and the identification among followers based on possession of a common trait recalls the child's consciousness of and reaction to the anatomical distinctions between the sexes. Throughout *Group Psychology*, Freud emphasizes the theory of infantile sexuality as a vehicle for understanding certain group phenomena such as suggestibility and what Wilfred Trotter called the herd instinct or gregariousness (117–121).

In *Totem and Taboo* Freud develops a stage theory of "human views of the universe," or *Weltanschauungen*. He introduces this theory by saying: "The human race, if we are to follow the authorities, have in the course of the ages developed three such systems of thought—three great pictures of the universe: animistic (or mythological), religious and scientific." "Animism" Freud uses to mean "the doctrine of souls," and, in its widest meaning, "the doctrine of spiritual beings in general." He says that this doctrine has three major parts: (1) belief that the world is populated by "innumerable spiritual beings both benevolent and malignant"; (2) belief that these spiritual beings are the cause of natural phenomena; (3) belief that human individuals are also inhabited by spiritual beings of this sort. Animism is a system of thought; it "allows us to grasp the whole universe as a single unity from

156

a single point of view."[19] The same can be said of the second stage of the human view of the universe, the religious. Freud does not deal with this stage at any length, but he does emphasize its close connections with animism: "With these three stages in mind," he says, "it can be said that animism itself is not yet a religion but contains the foundations on which religions are later built."[20] In the religious phase the view that objects are animated by spirits is modified into a view that there are certain chief or fundamental spirits and then into a belief in a single all-powerful spirit. The scientific stage, Freud says, contains the rejection of spiritism and a resignation to the necessities of nature. The interconnections of these stages are clear when Freud discusses them in relation to "omnipotence of thoughts":

> At the animistic stage men ascribe omnipotence to *themselves.* At the religious stage they transfer it to the gods but do not seriously abandon it themselves, for they reserve the power of influencing the gods in a variety of ways according to their wishes. The scientific view of the universe no longer affords any room for human omnipotence; men have acknowledged their smallness and submitted resignedly to death and to the other necessities of nature. None the less some of the primitive belief in omnipotence still survives in men's faith in the power of the human mind, which grapples with the laws of reality.[21]

Freud goes on to make an analogy between these stages and the stages of sexuality. The animistic stage corresponds to the narcissistic. In both, the thoughts and wishes of the person are regarded as successful deeds; the necessities of reality are not considered. The religious stage corresponds to that point in the child's development when he establishes object relations with the parents. The words "God the father" for Freud point to the early dependent relations with the parents. The scientific stage corresponds to the genital phase

[19] Freud, *Totem and Taboo, SE,* xiii, 77, 75, 76, 77.
[20] Ibid., 77
[21] Ibid., 88.

of development, in which the person attempts to satisfy his desires in the external world. In the scientific stage the person takes the necessities of nature—and of these Freud wants to emphasize death above all—into account in his attempts at satisfaction.

Our reading of the stage theory as dialectical holds at the group level as well. The animistic phase does not perish completely, but survives in some form in the following stages. Freud explicitly points this out in saying that "the primitive belief in omnipotence survives in men's faith in the power of the human mind." He also notes that the "human being remains to some extent narcissistic even after he has found external objects for his libido."[22] The belief in spirits, characteristic of both the animistic and the religious stages, constitutes a recognition of necessity at the expense of human narcissism. This recognition forms the main component of the scientific stage:

> If the survivor's position in relation to the dead was really what first caused primitive man to reflect, and compelled him to hand over some of his omnipotence to the spirits and to sacrifice some of his freedom of action, then these cultural products would constitute a first acknowledgement of *Ananke* [Necessity] which opposes human narcissism. Primitive man would thus be submitting to the supremacy of death with the same gesture with which he seemed to be denying it.[23]

The submission to the supremacy of death is preserved in the development to the scientific stage. At the group level, then, the early stages are negated and preserved, and do not perish in the course of its changes.[24]

---

[22] Ibid., 89.

[23] Ibid., 93. The editors of the *Standard Edition* put "Necessity" in brackets.

[24] Freud spent a great deal of time investigating the psychological components of religion and often compared religion and science. His strong attacks against religion complicate, but do not undercut, the reading of the stage theory presented here. The most complete account of Freud's views on religion is *The Future of an Illusion* (1927), *SE*, xxi, 3–56. See also: "Obsessive Actions and Religious Practices" (1907), *SE*, ix, 115–128; "A Religious

In the first section of this work I emphasized the function of sexuality as limiting psycho-analysis to the mental. When Freud gave up the search for indications of reality—when he gave up the "seduction theory"—he had recognized that the domain of psycho-analysis was the mind and its meanings. Freud's reactions to the "historic deed," and, in particular, the "primal deed," are in many ways analogous to his reaction to "the scene of seduction." In his recognition that the task of the psycho-analytic study of the group was to bring meaning to the history of signs in the present, and not to enumerate facts of the past, one sees the parallel to the limit of psycho-analysis to the mental in the theory of sexuality.

The first work to examine here is *Totem and Taboo* because in this text Freud's search for origins and indications of reality seems almost obsessive. The work ends with a quote from Goethe's *Faust*: "in the beginning was the Deed."[25] The reader may view this apparent search for origins as a remnant of the positivist or empiricist in Freud, or even as evidence of his having never fully given up the seduction theory.[26] The case of the Wolf Man, published five years after *Totem and Taboo*, seems to show this search for origins as well.[27] Readings that emphasize Freud's reliance on indica-

---

Experience" (1928), *SE*, xxi, 167–171; *Civilization and Its Discontents* (1930), *SE*, xxi, especially 64–85; *New Introductory Lectures on Psycho-Analysis* (1933), *SE*, xxii, 158–182 (Lecture xxxv); and *Moses and Monotheism* (1939), *SE*, xxiii, 3–137. See also above, note 7.

[25] *Totem and Taboo*, *SE*, xii, 161. From Goethe's *Faust*, Book I, l.1237.

[26] Recently, Jeffrey M. Masson has tried both to stir up some scandal and to revive the seduction theory in *The Assault on Truth: Freud's Suppression of the Seduction Theory* (New York, 1984). Janet Malcolm provides a lively account of much of the scandal and some of the issues it raises in *In the Freud Archives* (New York, 1984). In a much more serious way, Clark Glymour sees remnants of the seduction theory still operative in Freud's "Rat Man" case; see his "Freud, Kepler and the Clinical Evidence," in *Freud: A Collection of Critical Essays*, ed. Richard Wollheim (New York, 1974), 285–304; and, more generally, his "The Theory of Your Dreams," in *Physics, Philosophy and Psychoanalysis: Essays in Honor of Adolf Grünbaum* (Dordrecht, 1983), 57–71. For an intelligent historical account, see William McGrath, *Freud's Discovery of Psychoanaylsis: The Politics of Hysteria* (Ithaca, 1986), passim.

[27] *From the History of an Infantile Neurosis*, *SE*, xvii, especially 89–103.

tions of reality are often more concerned, however, with what they take to be Freud's personal feelings or idiosyncrasies than they are with the theory he originated.[28] In this section, I shall try to show the *theoretical function* of this search for origins in *Totem and Taboo*. By grasping this function we shall gain a better understanding of how psycho-analysis as a theory of history makes meaning out of memory and the absence of memory, and does not aim to reconstruct the past "as it really was."

Freud concludes *Totem and Taboo* with an affirmation of a historical deed, after having considered that the deed could have been merely a psychical wish. That is, he considers and rejects the explanation that the primal crime could have taken place in the imagination only; he does not blindly assume that there must be an actual deed at the roots of the oedipal situation. The reasons he gives for rejecting the psychical interpretation are crucial. The primitives, according to Freud, live in an animistic phase in which they attribute omnipotence to their thoughts. That is, whatever happens to objects in ideas, happens to what one might call the objects-themselves. This belief is similar—and Freud points out the similarity—to the obsessional neurotic's fear that his thoughts about the future of persons will become the reality of these persons. The obsessive will feel an immense guilt, then, over his thoughts. Yet although the similarity between the obsessive and the primitive is great in this regard, the process is not identical for both. "It is no doubt true that the sharp contrast that *we* make between thinking and doing is absent in both of them," Freud writes. "But neurotics are above all *inhibited* in their actions: with them the thought is a complete substitute for the deed. Primitive men, on the other hand, are *uninhibited*: thought passes directly into action. With them it is rather the deed that is a substitute for the thought." This essential difference between the character of the obsessive

---

[28] See, for example, even the exceptionally intelligent article by Jean Laplanche and J.-B. Pontalis, "Fantasy and the Origins of Sexuality," *IJP*, 49 (1968), 1–18.

and that of the primitive leads Freud to conclude: "And that is why, without laying claim to any finality of judgement, I think that in the case before us it may safely be assumed that 'in the beginning was the Deed.' "[29]

Although Freud does not blindly assume that there must be an actual deed at the root of the Oedipus complex, his view that a primal crime did in fact occur may be bound up with a belief that the psychical must ultimately have a base in the actual or experiential. His remarks on the conclusions that he reached in *Totem and Taboo* are instructive here. He warns the reader of what is to come in a footnote at the beginning of the last essay of the work: "The determination of the original state of things thus invariably remains a matter of construction."[30] A construction for Freud is not a meaningless or facile creation; it is a way to bring a series of disconnected facts together into a consistent whole.[31] He also uses another significant word to describe the status of the conclusions of *Totem and Taboo*. In *An Autobiographical Study* (1925), for example, he writes: "When I further took into account Darwin's conjecture that men originally lived in hordes, each under the domination of a single, powerful, violent and jealous male, there arose before me out of all these components the following hypothesis, or, I would rather say, vision."[32] Calling the primal horde and the killing of the father a construction, a vision, makes Freud's insistence on the deed at the close of *Totem and Taboo* more ambiguous and more difficult. In *Civilization and Its Discontents* he again returns to the question of whether the brothers must have committed the parricide, or might have just wished it to occur:

We cannot get away from the assumption that man's sense of guilt springs from the Oedipus complex and was acquired at

[29] *Totem and Taboo*, SE, XIII, 161.
[30] Ibid., 103n.
[31] In the *Future of an Illusion*, Freud describes *Totem and Taboo* as bringing a number of very remarkable, disconnected facts into a consistent whole; SE, XXI, 23. See also "Constructions in Psycho-Analysis" (1937), SE, XXIII, 255–269, where "construction" is given a more technical sense.
[32] SE, XX, 67–68.

the killing of the father by the brothers banded together. On that occasion an act of aggression was not suppressed but carried out; but it was the same act of aggression whose suppression in the child is supposed to be the source of his sense of guilt. At this point I should not be surprised if the reader were to exclaim angrily: "So it makes no difference whether one kills one's father or not—one gets feelings of guilt in either case! We may take leave to raise a few doubts here. Either it is not true that the sense of guilt comes from suppressed aggressiveness, or else the whole story of the killing of the father is a fiction and the children of primaeval man did not kill their fathers any more often than children do nowadays."

He goes on to make the distinction between guilt and remorse. The latter presupposes a conscience that existed before the deed that initiates the onset of the feeling. As Freud says: "An instinctual need acquires the strength to achieve satisfaction in spite of the conscience, which is after all, limited in strength; and with the natural weakening of the need owing to its having been satisfied, the former balance is restored."[33] The remorse that the brothers felt after they had committed the crime resulted from their "primordial ambivalence of feeling" toward the father. They loved their father as well as hated him; before the crime these feelings existed in a "balance of power." Only the aggressive instinct toward the father could be satisfied in a definitive way. Only through aggression could the father who persecuted and was loved become the dead father, the absent father. In this way he was placed beyond the reach of the deed, but was retained as an object for emotional attachment. The father is retained as the superego by means of identification,[34] he becomes the totem by means of displacement. The brothers could love the absent father more safely than they could the ruling father.[35] Freud is now able to answer the question he had ear-

[33] *SE*, xxi, 131, 132.

[34] Freud was using the term "super-ego" in 1930 when *Civilization and Its Discontents* was published. The term replaces "ego-ideal." See above, note 28.

[35] Compare this process with the way the little boy identifies with the father so as to escape his fear of castration and satisfy a portion of his

lier posed about whether the deed was essential for the creation of the sense of guilt. "Whether one has killed one's father or has abstained from doing so is not really the decisive thing," he says. "One is bound to feel guilty in either case, for the sense of guilt is an expression of the conflict due to ambivalence, of the eternal struggle between Eros and the instinct of destruction or death. This conflict is set going as soon as men are faced with the task of living together."[36] The essential concept at work in the primal horde hypothesis is ambivalence; it is the conflict of desires that is fundamental. Freud thought that the primitives would act from their ambivalence because they were uninhibited. The deed itself would become the origin of inhibitions.

The reader will no doubt remark here that by using *Civilization and Its Discontents* to gain an understanding of *Totem and Taboo*, I have merely shown that Freud grew less sure of his conclusions as time went on, and that he attempted to modify them. This, however, is simply not the case. In *Moses and Monotheism* (1937), for example, he reports that the conclusions he had reached in *Totem and Taboo* have only become more firm with time.[37] The preface to *Totem and Taboo* itself reveals the impetus behind the book and indicates how Freud viewed the status of the conclusions about the primal horde. He names two sources of stimulus for the work: Wilhelm Wundt's attempts to solve problems of social psychology through nonanalytic psychology, and C. G. Jung's attempts to solve problems in individual psychology with the aid of material from the domain of the social seen through an analytic perspective.[38] Freud clearly sees himself operat-

---

desire for the mother and father at the end of the oedipal period. Also, see Lacan's comments on the "Name-of-the-Father," the "symbolic Father" and the "dead Father" in "On a Question Preliminary to Any Possible Treatment of Psychosis," *Ecrits: A Selection*, trans. Alan Sheridan (New York, 1977), 199.

[36] *Civilization and Its Discontents*, SE, xxi, 132.

[37] *Moses and Monotheism*, SE, xxiii, 58. Other texts support the view that Freud remained confident of the conclusions of *Totem and Taboo*. See *Group Psychology*, 122–128; *The Future of an Illusion*, SE, xxi, 21–24.

[38] Wundt's work of 1912, *Elemente der Volkerpsychologie*, trans. as *Elemente of Folk Psychology* (New York and London, 1916); Jung's of 1912,

ing between the poles of Wundt and Jung. He will apply analytic psychology to problems at the social level.

The metaphor of acting as a bridge between Wundt and Jung is extended and deepened in the following paragraph of the preface. Here Freud comments on the deficiencies of his interdisciplinary and "pioneering" work. The essays that follow, he says: "seek to bridge the gap between students of such subjects as social anthropology, philology and folklore on the one hand, and psycho-analysis on the other." In the last two paragraphs of the preface the idea of providing the links between disparate elements is carried still further in an important way. The separate poles here are totems and taboos. The analysis of the latter is said to be exhaustive because the *taboos still exist for us today*. The mode of historical interpretation that was so crucial for individual psychology can be seen here again. Analysis starts from a sign that is present for us, the taboos, and proceeds to try to understand the history of that sign, that symptom: "The analysis of taboos is put forward as an assured and exhaustive attempt at the solution of the problem. The investigation of totemism does no more than declare that 'here is what psycho-analysis can at the moment contribute towards elucidating the problem of the totem'. The difference is related to the fact that taboos still exist among us." The analysis of the totem, although incomplete, follows the taboo analysis in form. In other words, the "slightest traces" of totemism that survive in contemporary religions serve as the basis for inquiry, as do the vestiges of totemism that can be seen in the behavior of children: "An attempt is made in this volume," Freud writes, "to deduce the original meaning of totemism from the vestiges remaining of it in childhood—from the hints of it which emerge in the course of the growth of our own children."[39]

Wandlungen und Symbole der Libido, and 1913, "Versuch einer Darstellung der psychoanalytischen Theorie" (in English in vol. 5 and 4 of Jung's *Collected Works*).

[39] *Totem and Taboo, SE,* xiii, xiii–xv. In *An Autobiographical Study,* Freud credits Ferenczi with a "lucky observation" of the "infantile return of totemism." See *SE,* xx, 67.

The bridge between the analysis of the totem and the taboo, we can see, is the story of the primal horde. It is a bridge between two interpretations that seek to bring meaning to the history of signs in the present. It is a construction; a vision of the way in which the histories of the vestiges of totemism and of taboos can be made coherent in relation to each other. The linked interpretations yield the "scientific myth" of the primal horde.[40]

From this investigation of Freud's treatment of the "primal deed," the analogy between it and the scene of seduction should be clear. Psycho-analysis remains, in both cases, concerned with the mental, with the mind and its meanings. The hypothesis of the primal horde is an attempt to find the meaning of signs that exist in the present in a way analogous to a construction's role in individual analysis. The concern of Freud's psycho-analysis is not to enumerate facts—not even facts which "tally" with "the real"—but to offer interpretations of the meaning of that which has been determined. The limit of psycho-analysis to the mental at the level of the individual is consistent with the application of psycho-analysis to the group.

IV

In the examination of the concepts of sublimation and the transference in Chapter 4, the distinction between the group and the individual began to become less clear. Sublimation, I pointed out, referred to the release of sexual impulses in nonsexual, *socially acceptable* forms. However, we also examined the connection between repression and sublimation, and the darker side of sublimation was exposed. Sublimation is the social mode of psychic defense, but, like all defenses, it is a denial of desire.

Although there is no detailed discussion of sublimation at

---

[40] Freud refers to the primal horde hypothesis as a "scientific myth," as well as just a "myth" in *Group Psychology*, 135, 140.

the group level in *Group Psychology*, there is an abundance of relevant material in the postscript to the work. As we noted above, Freud sees uninhibited sexual aims as being in direct conflict with the interests of the group, because they result in a pairing. Inhibited sexual urges, however, or urges that are detoured from attempts at immediate gratification, can be at one with the interests of the group. As Freud remarks in the postscript:

> Those sexual instincts which are inhibited in their aims have a great functional advantage over those which are uninhibited. Since they are not capable of really complete satisfaction, they are especially adapted to create permanent ties; while those instincts which are directly sexual incur a loss of energy each time they are satisfied, and must wait to be renewed by a fresh accumulation of sexual libido, so that meanwhile the object may have changed. [139]

Although these inhibited impulses can lead to a more purely sexual object choice which would be in opposition to the group tie, *as inhibited* these impulses are essential to the group. "All the ties upon which a group depends," Freud says, "are of the character of instincts that are inhibited in their aims" (140).

Sexual impulses that are inhibited in their aims are sublimated sexual impulses. The group depends, then, on the process of sublimation for its continued existence. The questions that now press for an answer are: what is the nature of the inhibition, and what are the costs of the inhibition that enables one to participate in a group?

Some preliminary answers can be sketched out on the basis of *Group Psychology*. Freud, as was seen above, makes an explicit connection between the demands of the group and the demands of neurosis. He points out that where a "powerful impetus" for the formation of a group appears, "neuroses may diminish and, at all events temporarily, disappear" (142). In commenting on the role that religions play in protecting believers from neurosis, he says that "all the ties that

166

bind people to mystico-religious or philosophico-religious sects and communities are expressions of crooked cures of all kinds of neuroses. All of this is correlated with the contrast between directly sexual impulses and those which are inhibited in their aims" (142). The "crooked cure" offered by religions is not a cure based on conscious choice, but rather, one based on unconscious processes much like symptom formation. This process is a characteristic not only of religious groups, however, but of groups in general. Freud comments on the way the neurotic, if he is not part of a group, recreates group features in a private from: "If he is left to himself, a neurotic is obliged to replace by his own symptom formations the great group formations from which he is excluded. He creates his own system of delusions, and thus recapitulates the institutions of humanity in a distorted way" (142). The connection then, between the creations of the group as a result of sublimation and the creations of the neurotic as a result of repression is an intimate one. The distinction between the two, however, is central. The neurotic's symptoms, like the group's manifestations, are the expressions of conflict. The symptoms of the neurotic, though, do not provide the same release of tension, the satisfaction, that the expressions of the group allow. The neurotic lives in pain in spite of his symptoms; the member of the group, one may say, escapes pain because of his symptoms.

This distinction soon becomes problematic, however. That is, as the expressions of the group stop providing the necessary release for its members, the differences between the psychological function of the group and of neurosis begins to erode (142). In *Civilization and Its Discontents*, Freud examines why civilization has progressed without a corresponding growth in human happiness. He reiterates the opposition between the group and uninhibited sexual ties, as well as the notion that civilization is based upon a renunciation of instinct.[41] A factor of utmost importance in *Civilization and Its Discontents* is the impulse toward aggression,

[41]*SE*, xxi, 97.

which Freud had for some time viewed as a manifestation of the death instinct.[42] Civilization is seen as a process humanity undergoes—a process that modifies the demands of instinct. Three results of changes in the erotic instincts are mentioned: character traits (of the group), sublimations (art, science, ideology), and renunciation.[43] Civilization also rests on a repudiation and a manipulation of the impulse toward aggression. It rechannels this aggression by monopolizing it and using it for the purposes of the group. In other words, the group finds other groups it can use to satisfy this impulse toward destruction; it makes war on them, or persecutes them through structured internal violence. As Freud says:

> It is clearly not easy for men to give up the satisfaction of this inclination to aggression. They do not feel comfortable without it. The advantage which a comparatively small cultural group offers of allowing this instinct an outlet in the form of hostility against intruders is not to be despised. It is always possible to bind together a considerable number of people in love, so long as there are other people left to receive the manifestations of their aggressiveness.

Civilization, he goes on to say, is a middle ground between desire and necessity. "Civilized man," he tells the reader, "has exchanged a portion of his possibilities of happiness for a portion of security."[44] The necessities of life are, in many ways, met by civilization; the fear of their being denied to the person is minimized by the basic guarantee that civilization provides. The cost of this guarantee must still be determined. Freud makes the precarious position of civilization clear before he explicates that cost:

---

[42] Freud published *Beyond the Pleasure Principle*, which developed the concept of the death instinct, in 1920. In this work, the impulse toward aggression is seen as a manifestation of the death instinct: *SE*, xviii, 53–55. See also: *The Ego and the Id* (1923), *SE*, xix, 54; *Group Psychology*, 102; *Civilization and Its Discontents*, *SE*, xxi, 117–122.

[43] *Civilization and Its Discontents*, *SE*, xxi, 97.

[44] Ibid., 114, 115.

And now, I think, the meaning of the evolution of civilization is no longer obscure to us. It must present the struggle between Eros and Death, between the instinct of life and the instinct of destruction, as it works itself out in the human species. This struggle is what all life essentially consists of, and the evolution of civilization may therefore be described as the struggle for the life of the human species. And it is this battle of the giants that our nurse-maids try to appease with their lullaby about Heaven.[45]

After concluding that civilization is the balance between the forces of Eros and those of Death, Freud goes on to examine the genesis of guilt and the relationship between guilt and remorse that was discussed above. After the reexamination of the story of the primal horde and the killing of the father, Freud concludes that guilt is an essential ingredient in any community of persons:

> What began in relation to the father is completed in relation to the group. If civilization is a necessary course of development from the family to humanity as a whole, then—as a result of the inborn conflict arising from ambivalence, of the eternal struggle between the trends of love and death—there is inextricably bound up with it an increase of the sense of guilt, which will perhaps reach heights that the individual finds hard to tolerate.

The cost of civilization, then, is "a loss of happiness through the heightening of the sense of guilt." Sublimation is a product of the conflict of desires which is fundamental to the group as well as to the individual. Guilt does not arise from any specific deed, but from this ambivalence.[46] There can be no "solution" to the ambivalence because the conflict itself structures our histories. Civilization is the outcome of this conflict: a compromise formation much the same—"economically"—as a neurotic symptom. Guilt is the price of this

---

[45] Ibid., 122.
[46] Ibid., 133, 134, 137.

conflict because desires remain in opposition; desires are both satisfied and denied in the course of group activities.

In the theory of the individual, guilt results from the severity of the superego. It arises from the failure of the person to live up to the high expectations of this agency, which is modeled on the idealized perception of the parents, as I noted earlier. At the group level, Freud postulates a "cultural superego," which would cause a societal sense of guilt because of the group's failure to meet cultural standards.[47] Sublimations are attempts to meet these standards (for instance, ethics, aesthetics), and, when they are successful in doing so, the *sublimations themselves become the new standards of the group.* Although there seems to be progress in civilization because of the great accomplishments that result from sublimation, the fact that these very accomplishments contribute to the heightening of the sense of guilt has been, Freud says, largely ignored. The failure to apprehend this darker side of sublimation—this subtle, but deep, form of repression—is one of the reasons why Freud chooses to speak of an "unconscious sense of guilt."[48]

Sublimation, then, plays an almost diabolical role in the history of civilization. On the one hand, it is a vehicle for minimizing the pain that results from the conflict of desires. On the other hand, it is a vehicle for the deepening of that pain in later conflicts. Not only is sublimation the shadow of a dream because of the gratification which it is incapable of providing, it is the deepening of a historical nightmare from which there seems no chance of awaking.

The examination of sublimation at the group level seems to leave little room for the extension of the previous interpretation of Freud's writings on the transference phenomenon. The exposition of the "diabolical role of sublimation" appears to have brought us to the depths of Freud's pessimism, and, if we take *Civilization and Its Discontents* and the other texts seriously, there seems to be no way out.

[47] *Civilization and Its Discontents*, SE, xxi, 141–144.
[48] Ibid., 133–144.

V

Perhaps the concept of the transference can shed some light on just where it is that "sublimation" has left us. The most obvious example of a transferencelike phenomenon at the group level is the leader-follower relationship. As in the transference, in the leader-follower relationship the person takes another figure as his ego ideal and reenacts his childhood patterns of being. In *Group Psychology*, Freud makes the analogy between the transference that occurs in hypnosis and the behavior of the follower vis-à-vis the leader. After speaking of the way the hypnotist gets the subject unconsciously to concentrate his whole attention onto the hypnotist—in order to begin a transference with him—Freud continues: By the measures that he takes, then, the hypnotist awakens in the subject a portion of his archaic heritage which had also made him compliant towards his parents and which had experienced an individual reanimation in his relation to his father" (127). Freud connects the leader too the hypnotist because of the ability both possess to reawaken the archaic heritage in their subjects. He is explicit about the relationship between the two: "Hypnosis is not a good object for comparison with group formation, because it is truer to say that it is identical with it. Out of the complicated fabric of the group it isolates one element for us—the behavior of the individual to the leader" (115).

The most obvious, and the most important, distinction between the transference relationship in the analytic situation and the one that exists between leader and follower (and in hypnosis) is that the former is specifically geared to make use of the relationship to manifest the infantile ways in which the analysand acts in the world so that he can know them and choose how to continue to act. This purpose is necessarily absent from the relationship between leader and follower as Freud describes it. The hypnotic quality of the attachment would be destroyed if the follower were to become conscious of the relation.

The leader-follower relationship had, Freud says, been

looked at by those interested in social psychology from the perspective which views the leader as evil, as manipulative, and as leading a stupid crowd. There are important reasons for having taken this perspective: the prototype of the leader for Freud himself is the primal father, and Le Bon's group is not capable of thinking for any length of time.[49] On the other hand, one can legitimately consider the analyst as the leader of the search for meaning in the analytic situation. The analyst, one may say, is the prototype of the "good leader" in Freud's writings. He leads in service to the truth.[50] He leads, as was seen above, in order to help the analysand know the history of his being in the present. Although the analyst leads, he does so in order to enable the analysand to choose independently of this leadership. Recall that Freud warned the analyst against becoming a teacher or a model for the analysand and said that "he should not forget that that is not his task in the analytic relationship, and indeed that he will be disloyal to his task if he allows himself to be led on by his inclinations."[51] On the basis of this analogy with the transference in individual analysis, it seems that a good leader would utilize the transference with followers to deepen their consciousness as a group. Is the analogue to the reading of the transference presented in Chapter 4, then, a leader who would refuse to become a model or a teacher, one who remains an analyst of some sort?

The major objection that Freud's work itself raises to this description of "the good leader" is the following: there is no reason to assume that the leader could control his being perceived as a teacher, model, or ideal by the followers. Their efforts to so see him would be enormous. If the leader attempted to dissolve the infantile perception that the group

---

[49] Le Bon conceives of the group as inherently irrational. Leaders influence crowds by affirmation, repetition, and contagion, never by reasoning. See Le Bon, *The Crowd*, Book I, chap. IV; chap. III. See also Rieff, "The Origins of Freud's Political Psychology," passim.

[50] See Freud, "Observations on Transference Love" (1915), *SE*, XII, 164.

[51] *An Outline of Psycho-Analysis*, *SE*, XXIII, 175.

has of him he would remove the preconditions of his leadership. In other words, the leader would no longer fulfill the group's desire for an ideal to identify with, and the members would seek a new way to satisfy this desire. The question remains open whether the leader could in fact foster the group's eventual recognition of this desire and perhaps enable the members to choose to act in different ways. On the individual level, the analyst can manage the transference so that it leads to the negation of the analysand's infantile ways of being, but on the group level the difficulties seem insurmountable. The psycho-analytic investigation of the transference phenomenon forces one to consider carefully the possibility of effective leadership—leadership in the service of the liberation of the members from their automatic attempt to realize their desires in a leader. It also reminds one of the difficulties inherent in the conception of such leadership, and reinforces the perception of its profound dangers.[52]

Fortunately, the leader-follower relationship does not exhaust the possibilities for an analogue to the transference at the group level.[53] In the more meaningful analogy with the

[52] The problems involved with the concept of an "analytic leader" of a group have not been dealt with fully here. I move on to different concerns because they present a deeper analogy with the reading of Freud's theory of the transference that was presented in Chap. 4.

[53] Several psychoanalysts and psychologists have commented on the role of the transference in group therapy and group dynamics generally. The concept of group transference is used by W. R. Bion to signify a therapist/analysand relationship within the context of a group in *Experiences in Groups and Other Papers* (New York, 1959), 31–32. Erika Chance also sees the analyst/analysand transference within the group and tries to prove that it is similar to parent/child relationships: "A Study of Transference in Group Psychotherapy," *IJGP*, 2 (1952), 40–53. Leonard Horowitz explores the way a trainer reduces the transference onto himself and becomes more of a member than a leader. He applauds the apparent feeling of equality that results: "Transference in Training Groups and Therapy Groups," *IJGP*, 14 (1964), 202–213. Under the guise of going "beyond the transference," Cornelius Beukenkamp simply avoids the problems of the analytic relationship in "Beyond Transference Behavior," in *Group Psychotherapy and Group Function*, ed. Rosenbaum and Berger, 614–617. Yalom sees both transference and more "here-and-now" "interpersonal learning" in groups: *The Theory and Practice of Group Psychotherapy*, 191–218.

individual transference, *the object of the transference is the group itself.*[54] This analogy is an extension of Freud's work. It is an extension, however, that is consistent with the most important theoretical developments in his investigation of the individual.

Freud comments on the widening of the family into the community near the end of chapter 7 of *Civilization and Its Discontents,* "What began in relation to the father is completed in relation to the group." He is referring here to the sense of guilt that began in relation to the father, but the connections between the heightening of guilt and the transference phenomenon are crucial. He goes on: "So long as the community assumes no other form than that of the family, the conflict is bound to express itself in the Oedipus complex, to establish the conscience and to create the first sense of guilt. When an attempt is made to widen the community, the same conflict is continued in forms which are dependent on the past; and it is strengthened and results in a further intensification of the sense of guilt."[55] The widening of the

[54] S. R. Slavson has done extensive work on the transference, which he sees occurring throughout the group. He uses the term "multilateral transference" in this regard. See, for example, his "A Contribution to the Systematic Theory of Group Psychotherapy," *IJGP,* 4 (1954), 3–29. See also: Irving Berger, "Modifications of the Transference as Observed in Combined Individual and Group Psychotherapy," *IJGP,* 10 (1960), 456–469; and Henriette Glatzer, "Aspects of Transference in Group Psychotherapy," *IJGP,* 15 (1965), 167–171. Mark Farell sees the therapeutic experience in the group arising from the understanding and resolution of what he calls "multiple transference constellations," in "Transference Dynamics of Group Psychotherapy," *Archives of General Psychiatry,* 6 (1962), 66–76. Wolf and Schwartz see a variety of transference relationships within a group in *Psychoanalysis in Groups,* 27–36. Durkin is especially sensitive to the myriad of transference phenomena, extending from the transference with the "group-as-a-whole," to a traditional analyst/analysand relationship: *The Group in Depth,* 88–90, 144–205. Foulkes stresses throughout his work that membership in a group leads not necessarily to conformity, but can result in a rich development of individuality. The working out of transference relationships in groups has much to do with this development. See, for example: Foulkes, "On Group Analysis," *IJP,* 27 (1946), 46–51; Foulkes, "The Issue," in *Psychiatry in a Changing Society* (London, 1969); and Foulkes, *Therapeutic Group Analysis,* 108–109, 177–180.

[55] *SE,* xxi, 132–133.

family into the community results in the manifestations of patterns of living that are derived from early familial relationships. As in the transference phenomenon, the manifestation of these early patterns can result in a consciousness of them and their eventual negation.

Several problems quickly come to the surface in this description of the group as the object of transference. The first is that acting in an infantile way does not guarantee, or even imply, that the action will be a prelude to a deepening of self-consciousness. If such a guarantee existed, neurosis would necessarily be a vehicle for knowledge. The second objection comes from the nature of the group itself. The transference in a psycho-analysis is an isolated phenomenon that takes place outside of the analysand's everyday life. The transference enables the analysand to see the affinities and the distinctions between his activities inside the analytic session and during the rest of the day. If one thinks of civilization as "the group," as Freud is doing in *Civilization and Its Discontents*, it is difficult to imagine another group that could lie outside it. Although the constitution of subgroups—countercultures—at the margins of civilization as vehicles for significant change has been popular with political theorists since the triumph of the modern state, this path is not open to psycho-analysis. The marginalization of political change would be considered a symptom of "the group as civilization" rather than an escape from it. The third objection to transference at the group level as the self-conscious coming to terms with the past arises in the context of what is necessary to perceive the infantile patterns in present activity. In other words, does the transference demand a high level of intelligence, and is it thereby limited to only a small class of people?

Full answers to these objections will not be attempted here. I do not think that on the basis of psycho-analysis as Freud conceived it they are possible. Other traditions of social thought must be brought to bear upon psycho-analysis in order to make the complexities of the dynamics of group consciousness completely clear. However, some preliminary responses can be given on the basis of Freud's work. These responses are not answers, but they do help to define the areas in which problems occur in the application of psycho-analysis to the group, and point in the direction of possible solutions. They are attempts to grasp whether participation in groups can effect the radical sensibility of the post-trans-ference consciousness postulated above. If that sensibility is necessarily destroyed in the group, the psycho-analytic con-tribution to any theory of political action is small indeed. If, on the other hand, that sensibility is deepened by the rela-tionships that participation in group activity makes possible, then that contribution may well be essential for an under-standing of how meaningful political activity can take place.

The first objection to the concept of group-transference can be partially granted. Neurosis can be the prelude to knowing, and it is viewed as such within the psycho-analytic situation. The transference relationship in psycho-analysis is a neu-rotic relationship. The analytic situation calls up defenses in the analysand that are pathological, and only by a working through of these defenses can the analysis be terminated. That is not to say that a neurosis necessarily presupposes the neurotic's eventual knowing of the history that domi-nates his present. One must not, however, neglect the import of the psycho-analytic observation that the neurotic's symp-toms are the *expressions*, the signs, of conflict. These expres-sions, if one takes psycho-analysis at all seriously, are the key to the apprehension of the conflict and the freedom to act through knowing. These signs or expressions may not be perceived—that is part of what neurosis is about—but their existence reveals the possibility of acknowledging the con-flicts of which they are the result and points to the freedom to change.

This response to the first objection accentuates the sec-ond. The transference is not merely a neurosis; it is a con-trolled neurosis. The analysand is able to come to under-stand the history of the conflict that results in symptoms because the conflict is contained in the analytic sessions. If one takes the group as the object of the transference, and civilization to be the group, then it seems impossible to conceive of a way a relationship to the group could be contained. The relationship of analyst to analysand is juxtaposed to relationships outside of analysis. With what could one's relationship with the group as civilization be juxtaposed?

Although Freud is concerned with the relationship between the individual and civilization in *Civilization and Its Discontents*, he deals in that work with many other subgroups of which the individual is a member. His examples are of a person as a member of a nation, a political party, a religious group, and a socioeconomic class. The transference relationship that could take place at the level of these or other groups would be valuable precisely because the group would be one of the tightly interwoven strands that make up the fabric of civilization. The examination of the role of the individual in any group would be relevant to his role in the larger groups of which he is also a member. The distinction and juxtaposition between analysis and "everyday life" are crucial to the value that the transference has in individual analysis. The fact that the analytic sessions take place within the fabric of the analysand's daily life is crucial in making insights that arise in analysis relevant to the analysand's thoughts and actions. Similarly, the connections and conflicts among the various groups to which an individual belongs would necessarily play a part in any attempt to grasp the significance of one's *participation* in a group. The notion of a "psycho-analytic retreat" is entirely foreign to Freud's conception of the transference. The ideal value of a group transference would depend on its existence within the totality of the groups that claim our allegiance.

One of the important implications of viewing the group transference as taking place on a lesser level than that of civilization is that it places the problem of intergroup relations within the domain of the transference. In other words, the tendency of groups to define themselves by their relationships to nonmembers would be an important problem for persons working through a group transference. For example, a person examining his relationship with the group—

177

the way his desires are taken into account by the group—
would have to come to terms with the tendency of groups
with strong ties among members to be aggressive to those
outside their boundaries.[56]

The third objection to the idea of a group transference is
a familiar one. One of the drawbacks to the notion of sublimation as a way out of conflict was that it seemed limited to
a small number of talented people. Freud's belief that psycho-analysis demanded a certain intelligence and sophisti-
cation adds weight to the idea that a beneficial group transference would be possible only for those with high intellectual
abilities or the money to engage in group therapy. Most persons, then, would be unsuitable for the transference at the
group level.

The concentration on intelligence or material factors as the
criteria for the establishment of transference shifts the focus
outside the proper domain of psycho-analysis. Psycho-analysis has no conceptual apparatus for dealing with the question of a person's level of intelligence or wealth. *The only
criterion for the transference within psycho-analysis is conflict.* The transference investigates conflict, and it depends
on conflict for the insights that it is capable of providing. As
Freud said in the *Project for a Scientific Psychology* (1895)
and continued to say throughout his work, contradiction is
the impetus of all thought and action.[57] The conflicts inherent in group participation—conflicts based on the contradiction between the desires of the individual and the necessities
as seen by the group—as well as the problems of the intergroup perceptions and actions would provide suitable material for the group transference. Indeed, it is difficult to

[56] Freud points to this hostility to outsiders in *Group Psychology*, 98–99, 101, and in his comments on the "narcissism of minor differences" in *Civilization and Its Discontents*, SE, xxi, 114–116. Note that the problems of intragroup love and intergroup hate would give the group transference a sexual content. These problems would force the members of the group to examine the bonds of identification that tie some together and exclude others.

[57] *SE*, i, 361, 386–387.

imagine a large class of persons who could be labeled "unsuitable" on the basis of the criterion of conflict.[58]

And it is conflict that provides the motivation for the group to work through the transference. The role of the transference phenomenon at the group level is not dependent upon the appearance of a "conductor" who would lead the members to self-consciousness by pointing out that their participation came at the cost of an unnecessary and painful denial of desire.[59] The felt conflict among desires, and between desire and the socially acceptable possibilities of satisfaction, would motivate the group's members to seek solutions in common to the contradictions that govern their lives.

This conception of conflict as the motivation for working through transference relationships may seem to simplify unduly the paradoxical "therapeutic alliance" at the core of individual psychoanalytic treatment, and it certainly runs counter to a contemporary view of analysis as providing a framework for a patient's ego or self development. Moreover, "transference" is a clinical concept, and here we are attempting to apply it to nontherapeutic groups. Therapeutic groups may develop precise goals and in any case are created with the intention of confronting psychological distress. The groups we have mentioned in this section are constituted for quite other purposes.[60]

This objection to conflating therapeutic groups with other

[58] On the "minimum ego structure" necessary for entering into the transference, see note 50 in the previous chapter.

[59] As has been the case in even some "psychoanalytically informed" genres of group psychotherapy. For some summary material, see E. J. Anthony, "The History of Group Psychotherapy," in *Comprehensive Group Psychotherpay*, ed. H. I. Kaplan and B. J. Sadock (Baltimore, 1971); *The Leader in the Group*, ed. Z. Liff (New York, 1975).

[60] Peter Lowenberg has applied the concept of transference in an interesting way to a more or less nontherapeutic group—graduate students—in *Decoding the Past: The Psychoanalytic Approach* (New York, 1983). Dominick LaCapra uses "transference" in a much more general sense in his "Is Everyone a *Mentalité* Case?: Transference and the 'Culture' Concept," in *History and Criticism* (Ithaca, 1985); and "History and Psychoanalysis," *Center for Humanistic Studies Occasional Papers*, no. 5 (Minneapolis, 1985).

social formations is an important one, because it is derived from the objection to using psycho-analysis, which is based on a study of pathological psychological conflict, to understand the workings of "normal" individuals, groups, and social expressions. Clearly, Freud thought that this extension of psycho-analysis was central to its claims on our attention and concern, and his work can be fully understood only as part of the tradition of modern European cultural criticism. Nonetheless, there are no real arguments that would legitimate attempts to understand the normal through a study of the abnormal, or to grasp the dynamics of culture through an investigation of its moments of crisis. The power of such a "method" is revealed only in its productions, in the coherence and force of the interpretations it provides.

There are, of course, important differences between therapeutic and nontherapeutic groups, just as there are important differences between what is called neurotic behavior and normal behavior. But these differences do not mean that the transference is confined to groups in which this phenomenon is discussed as such, or that individuals who are not in therapy do not experience transference. It is also true that within a therapeutic situation there is usually someone to steer experience toward the working through of transference, and that the presence of such a person can in no way be assumed in nontherapeutic situations. In stressing conflict as the motivation for working through transference, I have not tried to minimize the difficulties of this process of coming to terms with the past through the present. Instead, I have tried to show that outside the clinical situation the preconditions are still created—the painful contradictions of consciousness are reproduced—which may lead us to a shared search for a sense of the past that will not merely be a blind repetition of it.

The last objection to the idea of group transference seems to come from Freud himself. In *Group Psychology* he summarizes Le Bon's view of the group approvingly: "And, finally, groups have never thirsted after truth. They demand illusions, and cannot do without them. They constantly give what is unreal precedence over what is real; they are almost as strongly influenced by what is untrue as by what is true. They have an evident tendency not to distinguish between the two." And he continues: "Indeed, just as in dreams and in hypnosis, in the mental operations of a group the function for testing the reality of things falls into the background in comparison with the strength of the wishful impulses and their affective cathexis" (80). The possibilities for the transference are found in the conflict between the member's wishes and the necessities of existence. These wishes are confronted with the demands of the group as well as the contradictions between other desires that the member may have. The transference would consist in the member (as analysand) coming to know the meaning of his infantile ways of being vis-à-vis the group. The task of interpretation would remain with the member, but the group could act as a formidable vehicle for overcoming his resistance. This interaction between group and member could result in a manifestation of the conflicts of individual desire and group structure with the clarity that would be necessary to make those conflicts apprehensible.

The principal phenomenon of group psychology, for Freud, is the individual's loss of freedom in the group (95). The concept of group transference is a way for the person to find his freedom in a group. However, one must not lose sight of the reasons why Freud viewed group formation and maintenance as a renunciation of freedom. Groups, according to Freud, allow persons to manifest their infantile ways of being within a safe context. The psycho-analytic investigation of groups went on to analyze the desire that persons had to relate to one another by means of identification, the earliest form of object relations. Groups may tend to seek out leaders who will fulfill their members' need to act in relation to an ideal; they may punish all those members who dare to break away from the bond of identification and to act in nonconforming ways; they may not allow special meaningful relations to exist among certain members; they may be able to exist in harmony only by persecuting other groups, individuals, or certain classes of their own members. The group, though, offers the possibility of sublimations and the escape from the profound pain of neurosis. If the price of that escape is a loss of freedom, it is a price that many people are willing to pay.

Members of groups do not usually "pay a price" willingly, however; unconscious desires have been canalized or denied. The activities of the groups are an expression of those desires. The group, in other words, is the product and the expression of conflict. As the group fails to provide a release from that conflict—an escape from the pain of denied desires—the possibilities grow for its apprehension. The ambivalent nature of desire is exposed and intensified in the group. What began in relation to the father is completed in relation to the group. The transference phenomenon is the completion of desire, the grasping and knowing of desire. The conflict at the foundation of the group can be known because the group remains an expression of this conflict. If the individual loses his freedom in the group, the group still remains the expression of that loss of freedom. Through the group as this expression—through the transference phenomenon—the person can come to apprehend the meaning of his participation in the group and the potential for his activity within it. The group can know the costs, and possibilities, of belonging and participation.

I have remained on a very abstract level of discourse in this discussion of transference in groups. One can certainly imagine concrete applications of the idea of transference to group activity. Nationalism, for example, is, among other things, an expression of the infantile bonds of identification that can be manipulated and intensified by the creation of fears of insecurity. Insofar as these ties do not gratify members of a nation, and instead provoke conflicts in their values, the possibility of self-conscious change develops. A person plagued by a conflict between the values of two groups to which he owes allegiance—for example, one committed to social equality, the other to personal liberty—might come to see this conflict as a repetition of earlier conflicts in his personal and public life. Such a historical apprehension of the conflict would then inform his efforts to solve or avoid it.

Countless examples of how transference works at the group level can be generated, but they will not be all that helpful. Recognition of the occurrence of group transference alone is not sufficient for understanding the content of particular group conflicts, because psycho-analysis does *not* provide a sufficient theoretical basis for understanding life in common. For this task, moral, political or aesthetic criteria are necessary, and these, although they can be put in relation to the psycho-analytic acknowledging of history, cannot be reduced to psycho-analytic categories. An apprehension of the working of transference in groups can help one to sort out the conflicts among these criteria, but it cannot generate them.

The examination of the transference phenomenon in Chapter 4 showed that the end of analysis is freedom. Through an interpretation of the history of signs in the present, psycho-analysis enables the person to achieve a more complete self-consciousness than he had previously possessed. The person comes to understand how his history dominates his being in the world. The transference phenomenon, manifesting the contradictions in the life of the analysand, was said to lead to the creation of a radical sensibility, a sensibility open to acknowledging the roots of its present and its future possibilities. The question remained as to the potential for group freedom which would be necessary if a radical sensibility were to become more than an individual luxury; in other words, whether the potential for personal change through self-consciousness could lead to significant political change. The concept of group transference, the roots of which are to be found in Freud, is the vehicle for the creation of group freedom that would be analogous to the freedom found at the end of analysis.

Even during Freud's lifetime, psychoanalysts and social thinkers began to examine the political dimensions and implications of his theories. That is, they thought about our lives in common through the categories of dream interpretation, repression, infantile sexuality, and sublimation. My reading here, which privileges the concept of transference as a bridge between the psycho-analytic concern with the individual and that with the group, has drawn implicitly on this tradition of the political use of psycho-analysis. Perhaps it would best here to situate my reading in relation to this tradition.

Many of the political readings of Freud were certainly inspired by his own speculations on the group, which we have examined in detail in this chapter. Freud himself paved the way for subsequent analysts and social thinkers who saw in psycho-analysis a theory that revealed the dynamics of group consciousness and action, thereby increasing our understanding of how these relations are connected to our unconscious mental lives and making more possible than had been the case a conscious effort to change social relations. Although one should mention that Freud often rejected the social uses his followers made of psycho-analysis, it is clear that many of those who turned to his theories early on did so in part because of the ways these theories revealed fundamental aspects of political life.[61]

Perhaps the best known of these early political uses of psycho-analysis was Wilhelm Reich's. In the early part of his career Reich attempted to bring together Marx and Freud; he stands at the beginning at a long line of such attempts. The major historical dilemma that impelled Reich and others to attempt this synthesis was the rise of fascism. Why do "the masses" turn to fascism instead of communism? When historical materialism's answer to this question, based on an analysis of political economy, was deemed inadequate, psycho-analysis was brought in to reveal how a dynamic in "character structure" can explain why economic contradictions led to fascism and Nazism, and not to a proletarian revolution.

---

[61] An important example in this regard were the Berlin analysts in the 1920s. See Russell Jacoby, *The Repression of Psychoanalysis* (New York, 1984).

There is an enormous, and often helpful, secondary literature on Reich's work, and his contributions and errors need not be gone over again here.[62] In the terms of this study, we can say that Reich privileged the categories of infantile sexuality and repression and based his analysis of bourgeois society on the patriarchal family's repression of sexuality. He identified a liberation from this repression with freedom, rejecting the fundamental psycho-analytic notions of the necessary conflict in psychic life, and the irradicable ambivalence of our desires. In his later work, Reich increasingly depended on a biologistic notion of sexual desire, which, when released from social and psychological repression, would result in happy, healthy individuals. This work has little or nothing to do with psycho-analysis.

Other attempts to make Freud relevant to an understanding of politics that brought together psycho-analysis and Marxism were made by the thinkers of the Frankfurt School for Social Research. Like Reich, they concentrated on the family as a social unit crucial to shaping (and being shaped by) personality,[63] and they, too, turned to Freud in order to understand the failure of revolutionary politics and the power of the authoritarian state in the first half of the century. Eric Fromm's early studies, and the Critical Theory of Max Horkheimer and Theodor Adorno used Freudian concepts of conflict and contradiction to show the depth of change that would be necessary for social relationships to be radically remade. More recently, Jürgen Habermas has examined psycho-analysis as part of his attempt to articulate a concept of practical reason.[64] Marx's understanding of political economy, the Frankfurt School held, did not provide an adequate theory of modern culture and society unless it was complemented by a

[62] See, for example, Juliet Mitchell, *Psychoanalysis and Feminism* (New York, 1974), 137–226; Paul A. Robinson, *The Freudian Left: Wilhelm Reich, Geza Roheim, Herbert Marcuse* (New York, 1969), 9–74; Michael Schneider, *Neurosis and Civilization: A Marxist/Freudian Synthesis* (New York, 1975), 39–56.

[63] See their collaborative project, *Studien über Autorität und Familie* (Paris, 1936).

[64] Habermas, *Knowledge and Human Interests*, trans. Jeremy J. Shapiro (Boston, 1971), 214–300.

psycho-analytic conceptualization of the psychic economy that was produced by—and helped to reproduce—that culture and society.[65]

The best known attempt by a member of the Frankfurt School to bring out the radical political implications of Freud's work is Herbert Marcuse's *Eros and Civilization: A Philosophical Inquiry into Freud*. Marcuse was part of the Hegelian tradition of Western Marxism that privileged Marx's analysis of modern alienation and underlined the humanist and historicist thrust in his work. Marcuse turned to Freud for some of the same reasons that led Reich, Horkheimer, Fromm, and Adorno to psycho-analysis, but he finds there a revolutionary, even utopian, message.

Marcuse's "philosophical inquiry" finds a "hidden trend" in psycho-analysis. Since, he says, repression is the product of history, it may not be a necessary component of human relations.[66] Repression has many different forms, and these are always conditioned by the historical context in which they arise. Indeed, these contexts may even require particular types of psychological repression; but after the requirements—the historical necessity—cease to be valid, the repression may still be part of tradition, ideology, and culture. This unuseful, even dysfunctional, repression Marcuse calls "surplus repression."

With his concept of surplus repression, Marcuse succeeds in historicizing Freudian metapsychology. That is, he shows how the psychic economy of repression and gratification is mediated by the historical conditions in which individuals live:

[65] For a useful discussion of the Frankfurt School's use of psychoanalysis, see Martin Jay, *The Dialectical Imagination: A History of the Frankfurt School and the Institute for Social Research, 1923–1950* (Boston, 1973), 86–112, and passim. For a very critical discussion of revisionist uses of Freud in a political context, see Russell Jacoby, *Social Amnesia: A Critique of Conformist Psychology from Adler to Lang* (Boston, 1975).

[66] Marcuse, *Eros and Civilization: A Philosophical Inquiry into Freud* (Boston, 1955), 16.

The "body" of the reality principle is different at the different stages of civilization. Moreover, while any form of the reality principle demands a considerable degree and scope of repressive control over the instincts, the specific historical institutions of the reality principle and the specific interests of domination introduce *additional* controls over and above those indispensable for civilized human association.[67]

Eros and Civilization lays bare a dynamic in civilization in which archaic repressions that may have at one time been functional now are *only* repressive. By pointing out the ways in which this repression has come to be in contradiction with the development of civilization, Marcuse also points to the possibilities for liberation from these archaic inhibitions of desire. For Marcuse, it is the modern form of capitalism that perpetuates unnecessary repression; a real liberation of desire would make possible the transformation of society from the realm of Necessity to the realm of Freedom.

Although Marcuse's understanding of the dialectic of desire and history has been important for the reading of Freud I have presented here, the political content of *Eros and Civilization* depends on a notion of "necessary" and "surplus" repression that have no parallel in this book. Repression becomes surplus for Marcuse when technological progress has been sufficient to liberate us from the demands of alienating work. The contradiction between real progress and pointless inhibitions lies at the heart of the dynamic that Marcuse studies.[68] I have been concerned to point to the possibilities that psycho-analysis creates for the acknowlegment of contradiction, and the potential for self-conscious action—for freedom—that this acknowledging leads to. The transference has been emphasized as the vehicle for this acknowledging,

[67] Ibid., 37.

[68] Christopher Lasch, who follows Norman O. Brown in this regard, points to Marcuse's very problematic dependence on technological progress in his understanding of liberation. See *The Minimal Self,* 229–234. See also the fascinating exchange between Marcuse and Brown in *Commentary,* February 1967, 71–75, and March 1967, 83–84.

but I have not presupposed that a necessary condition for this realization is the objective presence of too much repression. That is, I have not argued that there is a *real* contradiction *prior* to the individual's or group's effort to make sense of the past; repression is interpreted as being "surplus" only by individuals or groups trying to make sense of their histories and capacities for the future, and is not judged to be *in fact* surplus by the social critic.

The other great radical reading of Freud in the 1950s was presented in Norman O. Brown's *Life against Death: The Psychoanalytic Meaning of History.* The discussion of sublimation above in Chapter 4 is heavily indebted to Brown's critical consideration of this social mode of psychic defense. Brown goes beyond Freud in showing how the individual escape from neurosis through sublimation can eventually lead to a neurotic civilization. Indeed, he sees the "progress" of modern civilization as the development of pathology.[69]

Whereas Marcuse accepted a great deal of civilization's accomplishments as providing the preconditions for a liberation from alienating work and frustrated desire, Brown emphasizes that society has turned from providing protection for the individual to becoming the chief source of suffering and the most important threat to existence. Recognizing that the survival of humanity has become a utopian hope,[70] he attempts to find "a way out" that would not result in the further desexualization of the libido and the additional buildup of frustration and aggression. Since this dual process has been, for Brown, the core of what is modernity, he does not depend on "historical progress" to solve the problems that it has engendered.

For Brown, the individual in modern civilization is no longer ambivalent. There is a desperate need, he says, to escape a civilization that may destroy all those in it. This escape, however, would have to be a flight from the structure of desire itself. Brown calls for the construction of a Dionysian ego, a

[69] Brown, *Life against Death: The Psychoanalytical Meaning of History* (Middletown, Conn., 1959), 143–144, 172, 174.

[70] Ibid., 305.

consciousness that would no longer negate, and that would freely experience satisfactions throughout the body. Civilization leads us away from the polymorphous perversity of our preoedipal existence. Brown wants us to find our way back to that wholeness prior to negation and history.

Although Brown explores the darker side of sublimation at great depth and with great incisiveness, in the end he calls for a consciousness that would not experience a conflict of desires, that would not experience ambivalence. He tells the reader at the close of *Life against Death* that what the world needs is "a little more Eros and less strife"[71]—quite a Dionysian revelation. The power of Brown's analysis of sublimation is great, but it leads only to this: a little more Eros and less strife. Of course, Freud (as well as almost anyone else) would agree with Brown here, but he would be concerned with how the psyche could live with this change, with what the costs of desire without conflict would be.

Clearly, even the title of my essay shows its critical distance from Brown's approach to Freud. I have emphasized throughout that psycho-analysis aims at a freedom that arises out of the possibility of a critical negation of the past; a freedom that comes through the self-conscious acknowledging of history. In this perspective, there is no way out of the ambivalent structure of desire. There is no possibility of gratification without conflict. Brown searches for a utopian hope because of his perception of a radical disease eating away even at our chances for survival. The reading of Freud presented here forecloses any escape from our histories and our desires, and instead aims to make a clearing in which the acknowledging and creation of a meaningful past will enable us to find the effects of our freedom in the present.

As I have noted at the end of Chapter 3, one of the most important political reactions to psycho-analysis has been that of feminism. Contemporary feminism, especially in the United States, has viewed psycho-analysis as one of the major pillars

[71] Ibid.

of the modern version of the patriarchal order. On the other hand, there have also been efforts to appropriate psychoanalysis for feminist use, or at least as a vehicle for understanding the dynamics of patriarchy.

This is not the place to rehash the many nasty things Freud said about women, or to juxtapose them with the few nice things he had to say. The efforts to make Freud more "egalitarian" by developing pseudo-concepts like "womb-envy," or to show that female psycho-sexual development is at least as good as male development, need not concern us here.[72] The happy hope that the idea of political equality may be derived from the study of children ignores, and can be ignored by, psycho-analysis as a theory of history.

Be seeing Freud as providing an analysis of patriarchy, and not merely being an expression of it, feminists have used psycho-analysis in the development of theory and interpretation. Juliet Mitchell's landmark study, *Psychoanalysis and Feminism*, successfully showed how Freud offers a theory of the production and re-production of patriarchy, regardless of his personal views about women.[73] This theory opens our

[72] For a particularly simplistic example of this easy egalitarianism, see Carol Tavris and Carole Offir, *The Longest War: Sex Differences in Perspective* (New York, 1977), 132–158. An extremely intelligent and critical appraisal of Freud's understanding of female sexuality (in boys and girls) is provided by Janine Chasseguet-Smirgel in "Freud and Female Sexuality," *IJP*, 57 (1976), 275–286.

[73] Mitchell's writings on psycho-analysis have been heavily influenced by Lacan's reading of Freud. See her introduction to Lacan's *Feminine Sexuality: Jacques Lacan and the Ecole Freudienne*, ed. J. Mitchell and J. Rose (New York, 1982). Lacan's idiosyncratic "return to Freud" has had a profound impact on French culture generally and on nonmedical psychoanalysis in the United States. In France since 1968, Freud has been appropriated by many thinkers on the Left, even while he has continued to be an object of criticism from all political parties. Those on the Left who are influenced by Freud, including feminists, often focus on his emphasis on the connections and disjunctions between the personal and the political. Lacan's emphasis on the role of language conflicts with some elements of my essay, but an appraisal of Lacan's importance is not my concern here. See, however: Sherry Turkle, *Psychoanalytic Politics: Freud's French Revolution* (New York, 1978); David James Fisher, "Lacan's Ambiguous Impact on Contemporary French Psychoanalysis," *Contemporary French Civillization*, 6, nos. 1–2 (1981–1982); *Returning to Freud: Clinical Psychoanalysis in the*

understandings to the historical dynamic of patriarchal power, without appealing to biological or economic reductionism. The sexist content it has stems from its hardheaded look at sexism. Psycho-analysis enables us to come to terms with unconscious forms of sexism, so that as the patriarchal order is transformed, we can find a place within that transformation for successful feminist political action.[74]

There is an important general sense in which the feminist reading/critique of Freud bears on the substance of the interpretation presented here. That is, a feminist reading of Freud derives its power from a concern with the ways in which the "personal is the political." As commentators have noted,[75] this slogan of the women's movement has an important resonance in Freud, whose work was focused on the connections between public life and the hidden realms of desire and its repressions. Rather than being a mere retreat from the political,[76] psycho-analysis makes its way "into the depths" in order to "shake the higher powers." Although it does not identify personal and political life, psycho-analysis can help us to understand the connections and the contradictions between them.

In this book, we have seen how psycho-analysis is first and

School of Lacan, ed. and trans. Stuart Schniederman (New Haven, 1980); Jane Gallop, *The Daughter's Seduction: Feminism and Psychoanalysis* (Ithaca, 1982); and Jane Gallop, *Reading Lacan* (Ithaca, 1985).

Part of the effect of the French turn to Freud has been a general use of psycho-analysis by philosophers, literary critics, and sociologists. For a good example of a thinker's use of psycho-analysis to discover the play of desire in the social realm, see Julia Kristeva, "Psychoanalysis and the Polis," *Critical Inquiry*, 9 (1982), 77–92.

[74] For a recent criticism of Mitchell and of Nancy Chodorow's psychoanalytically informed account of infant development, see Janet Sayers, "Is the Personal Political? Psychoanalysis and Feminism Revisited," *International Journal of Women's Studies*, VI, 1 (1983), 71–86. For an interpretation of psychoanalysis and feminism in the context of contemporary cultural criticism, see Lasch, *The Minimal Self*, 240–252, 294–297.

[75] See, for example, the article by Janet Sayers cited above.

[76] As Carl E. Schorske has argued brilliantly in regard to Freud's biography in "Politics and Patricide in Freud's *Interpretation of Dreams*," in *Fin-de-Siècle Vienna: Politics and Culture* (New York, 1980); see also McGrath, *Freud's Discovery of Psychoanalysis*, passim.

foremost a theory of history. I have concentrated on a reading of psycho-analysis, and have spent little time on the philosophy of history. It should be clear, however, that "history" here includes in a fundamental way the personal past, individual memory. In this chapter, we have seen that the concentration on personal history does not preclude, but in fact sets a base for, a consideration of a shared past, a collective attempt to find meaning and direction. The ongoing feminist confrontation with Freud has underscored that the personal past cannot be separated from a sense of political history. Indeed, that it is only by coming to terms with this dimension of memory and desire that we shall have a full understanding of the political.

Psycho-analysis cannot create a theory of revolutionary praxis. Freud's work can contribute to a theory of political action only through its perspective on the history of the individual and the group. Psycho-analytic theory, much like the transference phenomenon itself, is capable only of bringing into consciousness the contradictions that can lead to change. When the pain of these contradictions is known to be greater than the satisfaction derived from the group, meaningful change may occur.

The transference—both at the level of the individual and at that of the group—is a process for apprehending the history of one's activity and thought. The process results in self-consciousness, not in transcendence or redemption. Transference cannot destroy the past; it can lead only to people knowing the meaning of their history in the present. When this knowledge can be grasped, the conflicts that lead us to wish only in dreams and in fantasy may be effectively struggled with and not denied.

Index

Library of Congress Cataloging-in-Publication Data

Roth, Michael S., 1957–
    Psycho-analysis as history.

    Includes index.
    1. Psychoanalysis. 2. Freud, Sigmund, 1856–1939.
I. Title. II. Title: Psychoanalysis as history.
BF173.F8R72 1987   150.19′52   86-29192
ISBN 0-8014-1957-3 (alk. paper)